SECURE YOUR RETIREMENT

Achieving Peace of Mind for Your Financial Future

RADON STANCIL, CFP®   **MURS TARIQ, CFP®**

ISBN 978-1-09836-942-2 eBook 978-1-09836-943-9

Contents

MEET THE AUTHORS

RADON STANCIL, CFP, is a best-selling author and the founder of Peace of Mind Wealth Management, a firm committed to helping individuals retire with excellence. As the co-host of the *Secure Your Retirement* show, his insights have been featured in *Forbes*, *Newsweek*, Fox, ABC, NBC, and the *Wall Street Journal*. With over 25 years of experience, Radon is an award-winning advisor who is highly sought after by executives, business owners, engineers, pharmaceutical professionals, and more.

Radon's father was 52 years old when he was born. Growing up with an older father that was born during the Great Depression had a large impact on how he thinks. His father shared stories of what it was like to see a car for the first time and the privilege of having ice delivered to the house. Radon's father instilled in him a work ethic and taught him the value of saving for the future.

MURS TARIQ is also a CERTIFIED FINANCIAL PLANNER™ and a partner at Peace of Mind Wealth Management. With over a decade of expertise in retirement planning, Murs is dedicated to helping clients pursue their ideal retirement. As an author and co-host of the *Secure Your Retirement* show, Murs speaks on topics such as investing with risk management, income planning, and tax planning for and during retirement.

As a first-generation American, Murs was brought up with a different perspective on the value of a dollar and the importance of proper budgeting, saving, and overall financial planning. It is this upbringing that led him to his finance degree from North Carolina State University and eventually finding his passion in shaping the financial future of others.

ACHIEVING PEACE OF MIND FOR YOUR FINANCIAL FUTURE

For more retirement tools and tips for all facets of your future planning, make sure you listen to Radon and Murs on their popular podcast called *Secure Your Retirement.*

If you are nearing or currently in retirement, chances are that you want to make sure you have a rock-solid plan that is going to carry you through this next chapter of your life and ensure you have the money and freedom to really enjoy everything you've worked so hard for.

Retirement is the plan. You worked hard to get where you are; now it's important to have a retirement that works hard for you. If you want to achieve confidence, peace of mind, control of your future, a rock-solid income plan, financial freedom, and unrestricted options in retirement, the *Secure Your Retirement* podcast is the right one for you! Retirement is approaching, and you can't afford to make mistakes with your money. In the back of your mind, there are concerns about what happens if there is another financial downturn as you are getting closer to having the life you have always dreamed about. You have a desire for answers, but you tend to struggle to figure out what questions to ask. You possibly are frustrated by the lack of clarity on what to do and whether or not the advice you're getting can be trusted. Previously, you may have made the mistake of not doing enough diligence on who you work with and are cautious to explore another relationship. However, you know that if you don't take action and get clarity on your perfect retirement plan, you will be going into the most critical years of your life unsure that you are prepared to live out retirement as you've imagined. Radon Stancil, CFP®, and Murs Tariq, CFP®, are dedicated to guiding you through the process of knowing what questions to ask and what information to gather in order to feel 100 percent confident about your retirement plan. For more information visit: https://pomwealth.net/podcast or go to your favorite place to listen to podcasts and search "Secure Your Retirement" to gain access to a wealth of retirement planning tools and guidance.

ACKNOWLEDGMENTS

No project like this would be possible without the support of family, friends, and co-workers. We would like to thank a few people whose help was instrumental to this effort.

To our wives, Lauren and Taylor, and our children, Jackson, Bella, and Jai: Your patience in putting up with us is commendable under ordinary circumstances but was especially so during the progress of this project when you never once complained that we were spending too much time with the laptop. As always, our commitment to you is to endeavor to focus on the more important things in life and try not to let the everyday demands of our job rob us of the wonderful privilege of just being with all of you. It goes without saying, but it needs to be said here—Thank you and we love you very much!

Much of the facts-and-figures research of this publication was compiled with the help of our associates at the Raleigh, North Carolina, office of Peace of Mind

Wealth Management. These are professional people of the highest caliber, and we admire and appreciate their diligence and attention to detail more than they know. Thank you. You know who you are.

We also thank our loving parents for instilling in us the values of integrity, honesty, and hard work. They taught us that truth never has to apologize and always has its own license to speak and be heard. We hope some of that comes through in this work. Many of the privileges we continue to enjoy in our professional and personal lives are a result of what they taught us growing up.

Thanks also to our editors, Tom Bowen and Lars Dolder, whose help in producing this book is greatly appreciated.

PREFACE BY RADON STANCIL

The world in which we live is unpredictable indeed. Anything can happen, even the seemingly unimaginable. The morning of September 11, 2001, in New York City was clear and calm. At 8:00 a.m., millions in that busy metropolis were going about their business, tending to the affairs of what they thought was just another day. At that time of the morning, no one walking the streets of Manhattan could have known that suicidal Al-Qaeda terrorists had hijacked an American Airlines 767 passenger jet with the intention of crashing it into the World Trade Center.

Everyone remembers where they were and what they were doing when the tragic events of 9/11 unfolded. I lived and worked in Farmington, Connecticut, at the time. I had just sat down at my desk when my wife called and told me to turn on the TV. She said that a horrible accident had happened. A plane had just crashed into the north tower of the World Trade Center. I switched on the TV in my office, and soon the entire office staff was gathered around it to see what was going on. We all watched in horror as a second plane hit the south tower. And then we knew that this was no accident. The nation was under attack.

We closed the office, and everyone went home to call the people they loved. My wife's office was closed as well. We spent the rest of the day glued to the television, trying to wrap our minds around those horrifying events. Nearly 3,000 people died that sunny day, and the ripple effects of 9/11 have changed the world as we knew it.

A catastrophe of an entirely different nature occurred seven years later when the stock market crashed in 2008. This economic implosion also left those who observed it stunned and shaken—especially those who lost significant portions of their retirement savings. Like others in my profession, I'm sure, I watched the crawler at the bottom of the stock market channel on September 29, 2008, as the wounded and floundering Dow Jones Industrial Average, or as it is commonly called, "the Dow," bled out, losing a record 777 points in one day. But the troubles hadn't begun on that day, nor did they end there.

For years, the housing bubble had been steadily inflating to the bursting point. Developers couldn't build houses fast enough. Loans were easy to obtain, some requiring no proof of income or assets. They had been nicknamed "no-doc NINAs" by the mortgage industry, the acronym standing for "No Income

No Assets." Why would documentation be required? After all, what better collateral could you have than property that would always increase in value? At least that's what the lending institutions thought.

Then one day, the big banks that were behind the housing bubble were suddenly in the news. Banks that were "too big to fail," like Lehman Brothers and Bear Stearns, were going under. Each day that passed saw the Dow sink lower and lower. The optimists proclaimed on a daily basis that this time it had hit bottom and a massive recovery would soon begin. But it didn't. The Dow kept right on losing altitude. It couldn't go below 10,000, could it? And yet it did. On March 9, 2009, the Dow closed at 6,547.05, down 53.78 percent from the all-time high on October 9, 2007, of 14,164.53.

Those are just statistics. The human toll this financial disaster took could be seen in the ashen faces and worried expressions of those who had been hit broadside by the Wall Street crash. Some had lost as much as half of their life savings. Because I work mostly with people who are either in retirement or approaching retirement, I advocate an investment philosophy that simply won't allow those kinds of losses. The retirement nest eggs entrusted to my care remained intact through it all. Fortunately, when the storm winds of 2008 abated and things calmed down, all the retirement accounts I looked after were still there and had experienced minimal losses.

It is human nature to forget the bad things that happen to us after a while and return our focus to the good. Immediately after 9/11, we were happy to see those uniformed Transportation Security Administration people at all airport entrance gates. We happily removed our belts and shoes and emptied our pockets so we could walk through the metal detector without making a beep. We didn't mind the intrusion of our privacy. It made us feel safe. But a few years and scores of incident-free airplane rides later, we became less enthusiastic and more irritated by these routines.

After the 2008 market crash, a recession ensued that officially lasted until the third quarter of 2010. Some thought it was a generational economic crash, akin to the Great Depression of the 1920s. Surely, we'd learn from our mistakes and avoid such negligent behavior in the future. Unfortunately, there was never any basis for such short-sighted optimism. The events of 2008 came less than ten years after the dot-com bubble exploded in 2001. Now, as I sit at my laptop writing an updated edition of this book, we are again living through an unprecedented economic downturn as a result of the global coronavirus pandemic. Here's the point: the economy will always go through ups and downs—there's no room for complacency in investment. Former President Harry S. Truman once said: "It's a recession when your neighbor loses his job; it's a depression when you lose yours." Don't put off sound income planning when things are going well; that's exactly when you must shore up against the winds of change that will inevitably come.

WHY THIS BOOK IS IMPORTANT TO ME

I have had the privilege of being a part of the financial services profession for many years now. Over those years, I have seen many changes in the financial world. I have seen the rules and guidelines change. New strategies have come on line. All the elements that serve to shape our economic and financial landscape are in a constant state of flux. What does that mean? It means that if we are to succeed as savers and investors, we need constant and continuing education. If what worked last year doesn't work this year, we need to (a) know that as soon as possible and (b) be ready to shift gears. Our methods must be flexible.

That is why this book will not be a how-to guide or master plan. This will be no investment cookbook with fixed recipes and cookie-cutter solutions. That approach simply doesn't work in this modern age of market volatility and investment shape-shifting.

My purpose in writing this book is simply to prepare those who are now retired, or approaching retirement, with the education they need to enter this new phase of their lives with as little anxiety as possible. Retirement should be a comfortable time of life, not a period fraught with worry about one's finances.

I get hundreds of periodicals, brochures, and pamphlets each year from various investment firms and insurance companies, all dealing with retirement. I am always a little amused when I see the cover illustrations on all of this literature. The photos are usually of an older couple with salt-and-pepper hair, romping on a sun-splashed beach or holding hands in a meadow. Sometimes they play Frisbee with their grandkids. There is usually a dog in the picture too. I'm not sure who owns the dog, whether it's the kids or the retired couple, but the dog is a nice touch. Dogs, particularly Labrador retrievers and cocker spaniels, make us think happy thoughts. The people in the photograph also have radiant smiles—the kind usually produced by expensive dental work. There's no mistaking the inference—these pretty retired people have not one worry in the world. "I'm retired and loving it," they seem to say. The truth, however, is not always quite so pretty. Retiring can be a financial minefield, as the ones who lost half their fortunes in the 2008 market crash found out. You need a guide, a map to that minefield.

One aim of this book is to help you steer your financial ship past some of the rocky shoals that confront 21st-century retirees. As you thumb through its pages, you will not find a chapter in this book titled "The Most Wonderful Financial Product Known to Man." First of all, there is no such thing. Secondly, by the time you buy it, something would change, and it wouldn't be the "most wonderful" anymore. The precepts that govern what is and what is not prudent investing today may not apply next week. There is no silver bullet. Our approach must be broad-based. Therefore, we will discuss the merits and details of investing philosophies and retirement income planning strategies here, not quick-fix solutions.

You also will not find a chapter titled "Tax Loopholes to Help You Beat the Government's Tax Plan." The last I heard, tax evasion is illegal. You will, however, find some legitimate strategies that are fully endorsed by Uncle Sam that may help you avoid paying more than your fair share of taxes. As a matter of fact, Uncle Sam offers these strategies free of charge. He just doesn't advertise them.

So this book, as you will see if you keep reading, is basically a source of financial education. Knowledge can protect and empower us as we cut the umbilical paycheck cord of the workaday world and confidently enter the self-sustaining, pay-ourselves zone of retirement.

Every Situation Is Different

Family circumstances and the financial planning solutions that match them are as individual as fingerprints. No two are alike—not even in the case of identical twins, who, even though they share the same DNA, still have unique fingerprints. Just as doctors must see you and examine you personally before they prescribe a course of treatment or specific medication, a personal approach is needed when it comes to financial planning. Your retirement plan will be different from that of your neighbor, co-worker, uncle, brother, sister, or any other human being.

Did I say that all family situations are unique? My father, for example, was born on October 14, 1919. He was 52 years old when I was born. I have a younger brother who was born when Dad was 55 and a younger sister who came into this world when my father was 57! Here's where it gets a little complicated: My mother is 19 years younger than my father. I have another brother who is 8 years older than I am. My mother adopted him in her first marriage, and my father adopted him after marrying my mother. My oldest brother is 30 years my senior. He is my half-brother from my father's first marriage. All but one of his children—my nephews and niece—are older than I am. On top of all this, my younger brother married my first wife's younger sister. You would have to say that my family situation is nothing if not unique!

Your family situation may not include a structure as unusual as mine, but it, too, is unique. You have your own goals, dreams, desires, and plans. Money means something entirely different to you than it means to your neighbor, friend, brother, or cousin. Some want to leave all the money they possibly can to their children. Others want to skip their children, for whom they may have provided stellar educations and who are now successful in their own right, and instead leave a legacy for their grandchildren. Still others may feel like the man who told me one day—in all seriousness, by the way—that on the day he dies, he wants to write one last check, and he wants that check to bounce with the words *insufficient funds* stamped on the back. It reminded me of that bumper sticker I see on motor homes occasionally: "We are spending our children's inheritance." Different strokes for different folks.

What is your goal? I don't know, but I will guarantee you that it is not quite the same as everyone else's.

We All Play by the Same Rules

You can't imagine, nor can I, a baseball player making a beeline for the second base after hitting the ball and then, when he is called out, trying to explain to the umpire, "That's the way I play the game." No, we must all play by the same rules, both in baseball and in the game of life.

That principle also holds true financially. We may have unique goals, but we all share the same rules. For example, how much money can you put into an IRA? There are rules for that. How much must you withdraw from your IRA starting at age 72? There are rules for that. We will cover some of those rules in this book. Call them commonalities in the world of money management. And, no, you can't tell the IRS that you would like to play by your own set of rules. It just doesn't work that way. What you can do—and you will see as you read on that I encourage you to do this—is *apply* those rules to best serve your individual financial situation. That is the tricky part, but this book will provide some guidance.

Each year I do several educational seminars where I meet people from all backgrounds and walks of life. After one of those seminars, a man approached me and began telling me about his unique situation. He had accumulated a very nice estate and inherited a sizable amount of money. To educate himself, he decided to go to school and take all the courses needed to become a CERTIFIED FINANCIAL PLANNER™. He did not take the exam and had no desire to practice financial planning. He merely wanted to understand the rules of the game and how they pertained to his newly acquired wealth. I was impressed with his dedication to obtain this knowledge. When he asked me for an appointment, I asked him why he wanted to talk to me if he had obtained so much education. He told me that he had come to the conclusion that the rules are always changing and that, while he knew more than most people, he still recognized his need for ongoing guidance. "It's like trying to hit a moving target," he said. He was right.

This book will not endeavor to hold the target still for you. First of all, that wouldn't work. Second of all, it sounds a bit risky for the target holder. What this book will do, however, is endeavor to teach you how to adjust your sights.

CHAPTER 1

Why *Buy and Hold* Could Kill Your Retirement Plan!

There are certain words and phrases you just don't want to hear from the professionals who are supposed to be looking after your health.

Expressions you don't want to hear from your medical professional are, for example,

"Oops!"

"This is really, really going to hurt."

And my personal favorite: "Nurse, I'm going to need a mess of towels, a vacuum pump, a Phillips-head screwdriver, some super glue...and get my lawyer on the phone."

If you expect the medical professional looking after your *health* to be competent and not to make mistakes, shouldn't the same be expected of the financial professional looking after your *wealth*?

Are you sick and tired of hearing the same flimsy excuses and bogus explanations from your financial advisor when you open up your account statement only to discover that you have lost money?

"Don't worry; just hang in there."

"It will come back; you just need to give it more time."

And my personal favorite: "Well, don't feel like the Lone Ranger. Everybody lost money in this last correction."

Shortly after the stock market crash of 2008, I interviewed a couple who told me that they had lost half of their life savings in that Wall Street debacle. They were in their early 60s and owned a small business. They had saved enough to provide them with a decent income in retirement. Their plans had been to wait until January 1, 2009, turn the business over to their son, buy themselves a small camper, and finally do some traveling. They felt like they deserved it. They had, after all, denied themselves many luxuries to build the business, provide a nice home for their two kids, and send them to college. They had always been self-employed, so neither had a pension. But they figured that if they were careful with their expenses, the money in their investment account, combined with their Social Security income, would enable them to maintain a relatively comfortable lifestyle in their sunset years.

Then the bottom fell out of the stock market. They watched in nervous amazement as the stock market tumbled 777 points in one day on September 29, 2008. This couple, perhaps like many others, had not busied themselves with the details of their invested assets. They left all of that to their financial advisor.

"Just hold on," their financial advisor told them. "The market always comes back." So, not knowing what else to do, they stayed put. You know the rest of the story. The market continued its downward slide, and nearly half of the money they were counting on for retirement income went poof in the wind like dandelion spores in a stiff breeze. Naturally, these trusting souls felt betrayed.

"What got me," said the man, "was when our broker told us the thing about the boats in the tide."

I asked him what he meant. The man explained how his financial advisor had, in an attempt to console them, offered them the illustration that when the tide goes out, all the boats go down. Then when the tide returns, all the boats rise.

"I know something about the tides," said the man, who often fished off the North Carolina coast. "This wasn't a case of the tide going out. The whole ocean disappeared!"

"Yeah, I can't believe he said that," his wife chimed in.

What Would They Say?

If you were to ask your current financial advisor how he or she did in 2008—and, more importantly, what their plan of action is for the next "2008" when it comes— what do you think the answer would be? Hopefully, you aren't asking for the first time right now as the market again plummets amid a worldwide pandemic and government reform with economics experts warning that, in fact, we may have already reached the next "2008." If your advisor says that over time, the market will go up—you just need to "hang in there" and stay invested—perhaps consider finding a new financial advisor. That's Wall Street doctrine: always remain invested, regardless of current conditions. It's bad advice for soon-to-be retirees.

The *buy-and-hold* ideology makes about as much sense as hanging from a tree limb until you can't hold on any longer. If you happened to find yourself in such a precarious situation, desperately straining, your grip weakening by the second, what would you do? While you still have strength, the smart option would be to pull yourself up or maybe to swing safely to a lower branch. But what if instead your buddy (who's watching safely from the ground) were to insist you not do anything to help yourself, but rather "just keep hanging on." You'd probably laugh at such ludicrous advice.

Without anyone coming to rescue you, what's the use in hanging idly? You can't hang on forever; you're just wasting valuable time until your body gives out and you fall.

When brokers advise you to "just hang in there," it makes about as much sense as your buddy's advice to keep hanging from the tree. It's unsustainable. Eventually, you won't be able to endure the market loss, especially if you're already retired and drawing from those funds. Inevitably, you'll "fall"—you'll have to sell out, probably at the bottom of the stock market.

You may be wondering why buy and hold is so often preached when it almost never works for aging investors. It's because the people saying it need you to stay in the stock market. It's their industry and they need clients. Can you imagine your mutual fund company ever calling to tell you, "Market conditions are bad right now, so it would be prudent to exit your fund and park your money in safety for the time being"? Didn't think so.

What if other industries did this? You would lose all trust and never use their services. For example, suppose you are talking to an airplane pilot who tells you, "I never pay attention to the weather. I just take off no matter what." I don't think you would ever board that plane! But the fact is, many people hand over their life savings to a financial advisor, money manager, or mutual fund company whose investing philosophy is that you should always be invested, regardless of market conditions. They trust these advisors to get them to their destination of financial security and adequate wealth for a worry-free retirement. Is that wise?

The History of Buy and Hold

What I am about to share with you in these next few paragraphs is an unpopular truth—unpopular, that is, among those who adhere to what is called the buy-and-hold philosophy of investing.

Personally, I hate the noise that sirens make. They are grating sounds that I wish would go away. But usually, they are warning me of something and telling me that I should take some action for my personal safety. I want you to see the truth about buy and hold so you can take action and do something different to grow your money and protect your portfolios from major decline.

Let's start with some history. For years now, most investors have been taught lies and fed false information when it comes to investing strategies. I am reminded of a famous quote by H. L. Mencken, an American journalist, satirist, and critic from over 100 years ago: *"The men the American public admire most extravagantly are the most daring liars; the men they detest most violently are those who try to tell them the truth."* Unpopular or not, I intend to tell you the truth and back it up with hard facts.

When do you think buy and hold works the very best? That's right; when you are in a bull market, that is, a time when the market is on an upswing.

Take the bull market that started in January 1990, for example, and continued through March of 2000. That was a bull stampede! It was a decade of virtually uninterrupted growth. The S&P 500 grew by an impressive 455 percent. Think about it in terms of cash. If you had invested $100,000 in January 1990 and just let it ride, your $100,000 would have been worth $455,000 by March 2000.

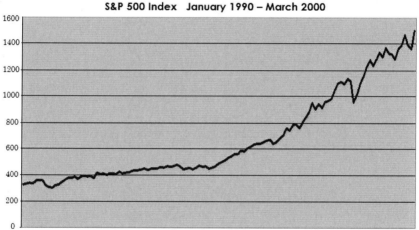

S&P 500 Index   January 1990 – March 2000

* The Standard & Poor's Stock Index (S&P 500) is an unmanaged index generally representative of the U.S. stock market without regard for company size and cannot be invested in directly. Past performance is no assurance of future results. The market for all securities is subject to fluctuation, including possible loss of principal.

The reason for the major expansion during this era was the staggering growth of individual stock ownership—from 15 percent to 55 percent. Why did that happen? Because companies were ditching their traditional defined benefit pension plans and moving to 401(k) plans. There was a tremendous influx of cash into the stock market during that decade. It came in one paycheck at a time from millions and millions of ordinary savers across the nation. Primarily, those dollars went to buy shares in mutual funds held by 401(k) plans. Buy and hold was king during this ten-year period. But what came next? The downside!

From March 10, 2000, to October 9, 2002, the market lost $9 trillion. The S&P 500 lost 49 percent, and the NASDAQ lost 79 percent. The average investor lost 47.4 percent.

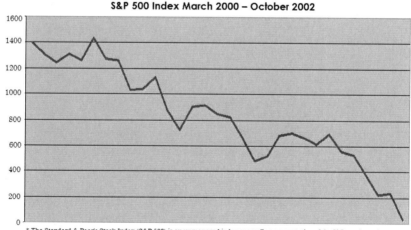

S&P 500 Index March 2000 – October 2002

* The Standard & Poor's Stock Index (S&P 500) is an unmanaged index generally representative of the U.S. stock market without regard for company size and cannot be invested in directly. Past performance is no assurance of future results. The market for all securities is subject to fluctuation, including possible loss of principal.

Again, thinking in terms of cash, your $455,000 would have dropped to $239,330 during this short two-year period. What did most advisors tell their clients to do? "Hang in there. Stay invested for the long term."

Another upside did happen. It was not as long and voluminous as the decade-long bull market of the 1990s, but it wasn't too shabby. From October 9, 2002, to October 9, 2007, the S&P 500 grew 102 percent. This means that if you had not needed to touch your investments from the prior downturn, your $239,330 would have grown to $483,446. If you had been in a situation where you had to withdraw money from your account, however, you would not have recovered.

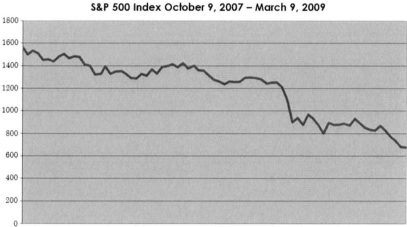

S&P 500 Index October 9, 2007 – March 9, 2009

* The Standard & Poor's Stock Index (S&P 500) is an unmanaged index generally representative of the U.S. stock market without regard for company size and cannot be invested in directly. Past performance is no assurance of future results. The market for all securities is subject to fluctuation, including possible loss of principal.

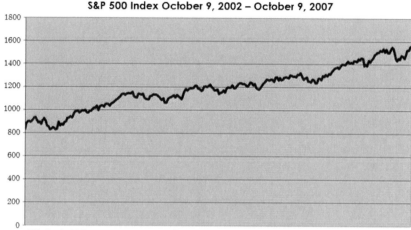

S&P 500 Index October 9, 2002 – October 9, 2007

* The Standard & Poor's Stock Index (S&P 500) is an unmanaged index generally representative of the U.S. stock market without regard for company size and cannot be invested in directly. Past performance is no assurance of future results. The market for all securities is subject to fluctuation, including possible loss of principal.

How could anyone have known what was about to happen next? Another bear market was coming! In only 17 months, from October 9, 2007, to March 9, 2009, the stock market lost more than the 2000–2002 crash! This red-ink gusher saw more than $11 trillion in losses, compared to the $9 trillion lost in 2000–2002. The tale of the tape was shocking. The S&P 500 lost 57 percent, the NASDAQ lost 52 percent, and the Dow Jones Industrial Average (DJIA) lost 57 percent of its value. The average investor lost 56.78 percent. Looking at it in terms of cash wealth, your $483,446 plummeted to $208,945 in 2009.

What Is at Stake?

It is devastating anytime you lose money that you have worked hard to earn and strived diligently to save. But if you had been in retirement or within a few years of retirement in 2000 or 2007 and experienced a 50 percent loss of your life savings, the impact would have been devastating. If you had subscribed to the buy-and-hold philosophy of investing, where would you be today? Even if you had earned a steady 10 percent per year, it would have taken you 82 months (7 years) to recover. If you had earned 5 percent, it would have taken you 161 months (13 years) to recover! And that's if you had pulled no money from the account to live on. If you had taken withdrawals from the account in question, the effect of the losses would have been amplified, and the recovery time would have been greatly prolonged.

Dispelling the Myths

The following is not meant to depress you, but to empower you. It's just like those sirens I mentioned earlier. Their sounds may not be pleasant, but they are useful. On May 20, 2013, people living in Moore, Oklahoma, heard the shrill, bleating sound of warning signals over their radios, televisions, and neighborhood sirens 36 minutes before an EF5 tornado tore through a section of town. With winds estimated at over 200 miles per hour, the mile-wide buzz saw left 23 dead and 377 injured. It would have cost even more lives had those precious 36 minutes not been available to those who grabbed what they could and left the vicinity.

During those dark days following the 2008 market crash, I felt like a financial first responder to many who, acting on the buy-and-hold mantra of their financial advisors, froze like deer in headlights and left their savings to the ravages of the storms battering the stock market.

Some who visited my office during that time had that dazed "what just happened?" look. Some of them told me what their current advisors had been telling them, and I started to notice a common thread to their statements. I found myself explaining to many of them why what they thought were sound principles of investing were, in actuality, investing myths. Here are some of the most common myths propagated by some in the financial advisory community and the truths that dispel them:

Myth #1: "It was a once-in-a-lifetime event. My broker says it won't happen again."

I'm sorry, what! If myths were continents, this one would be Asia. Let's be absolutely clear: *it* always happens again. But as investors, if we're not careful, we may be quick to forget the trend in favor of blind sanguinity. For many years now, I have always maintained that you should only work with an advisor who can explain in detail what he or she will do to protect your assets from the next bear market, not just what will happen during a growth phase. It's not the feel-good message of your average broker, but it's what you need for the sake of your retirement security.

A bear market, by definition, is a 20 percent or greater decline in the S&P 500 Index. In my profession, regulators do not allow us to make guarantees. But in the interest of overwhelming clarity, I will make this guarantee about bear markets—they are not once-in-a-lifetime events. They will happen again and again.

That guarantee is supported by Table 1 and accompanying facts.

Table 1			
S&P 500 Corrections			
September 1929 through June 2020 (90 years)			
Bear Market	**Duration**	**Decline**	**Time to Break Even**
September 1929 – June 1932	33 months	−86.7%	302 months
July 1933 – March 1935	20 months	−33.9%	28 months
March 1937 – March 1938	12 months	−54.5%	107 months
November 1938 – April 1942	41 months	−45.8%	77 months
May 1946 – March 1948	22 months	−28.1%	49 months

Table 1			
S&P 500 Corrections			
September 1929 through June 2020 (90 years)			
Bear Market	**Duration**	**Decline**	**Time to Break Even**
August 1956 – October 1957	14 months	−21.6%	25 months
December 1961 – June 1962	6 months	−28.0%	22 months
February 1966 – October 1966	8 months	−22.2%	16 months
November 1968 – May 1970	18 months	−36.1%	39 months
January 1973 – October 1974	21 months	−48.2%	91 months
November 1980 – August 1982	21 months	−27.1%	25 months

Table 1			
S&P 500 Corrections			
September 1929 through June 2020 (90 years)			
Bear Market	Duration	Decline	Time to Break Even
August 1987 – December 1987	3 months	−33.5%	23 months
July 1990 – October 1990	3 months	−19.9%	7 months
July 1998 – October 1998	3 months	−21.2%	3 months
March 2000 – October 2002	31 months	−49.1%	87 months
October 2007 – March 2009	17 months	−56.78%	65 months
Source: www.standardandpoors.com, www.yardeni.com			

Important facts to note:

- Since 1929, we have experienced 17 bear markets.
- The average frequency of a new bear market since 1929 is once every 4.8 years.

- The average depth of a bear market is a 38.24 percent decline.
- The average duration of a bear market is 17 months.
- The average time to make up a loss from a bear market is 60 months (5 years).

In about 54 out of 90 years (60 percent of the time), most investors have simply been making up losses. All new growth has occurred in just 40 percent of the time invested.

Myth #2: "I only invest in blue-chip companies. I won't get hurt!"

This investing myth is one that originates from our parents' and grandparents' eras. It is widely believed, but it simply isn't true. Look at the list in Table 2, and you will see companies whose products, services, and trademarks are well known. They are big names among the blue-chip stocks. Many of these companies are huge, yet note the losses they sustained in 2000.

Table 2		
Dow Component	2002–2003 Performance	Back to Even
Coca-Cola	−45%	2011
General Electric	−63%	Unknown!
Altria	−67%	2005
Disney	−68%	2011
Merck	−59%	Unknown!

Table 2		
Dow Component	**2002–2003 Performance**	**Back to Even**
Walmart	−40%	2012
Exxon	−36%	2004
Alcoa	−60%	2007
Home Depot	−70%	2013
Hewlett Packard	−84%	Unknown!
AT&T	−67%	Unknown!
Microsoft	−65%	Unknown!
Source: Dorsey Wright and Associates, www.dorseywright. com		
Performance data does not include reinvested dividend distributions.		
Updated through June 2020		

Myth #3: "If I only invest in diversified mutual funds, I won't get hurt!"

The preceding myth about blue-chip stocks also goes for mutual funds. If you look at the data presented in Table 3, you will see that many of the biggest mutual funds had major losses in the last bear market.

Table 3		
Mutual Fund	**10/9/07–3/9/09 Performance**	**Back to Even**
American Funds Growth	−52%	2013
American Funds Cap Inc	−43%	Unknown!

Table 3		
Mutual Fund	10/9/07–3/9/09 Performance	Back to Even
Fidelity Contrafund	–48%	2012
American Funds Cap World	–52%	2009
Vanguard Total Stock	–55%	2013
American Funds Inv Co Amer	–51%	2013
American Funds Income	–45%	2014
Vanguard 500 Index	–55%	2013
American Funds Washington	–54%	2013
Vanguard Inst Index	–55%	2013

*Source: Dorsey Wright and Associates, www.dorseywright. com

*Performance data does not include dividend and capital gains distributions or reinvestments.

*Updated through June 2020

*Prospectuses which contain details about the investment objectives, risks, charges, and expenses as well as other important information about investing in mutual funds are available. You should carefully read and consider this information prior to investing.

"Buy-Side" Bias: How Traditional Broker-Dealers Deal with a Declining Market

First and foremost, traditional broker-dealers do not have *sell-side discipline*. They rarely, if ever, suggest selling anything. On the contrary, they have a *buy-side bias*. They have every incentive to keep you invested no matter what. What would happen if your mutual fund company called you and said, "We feel this market has too much risk, and we feel you should sell your shares in our mutual fund company?" They would stop getting their fees! Arthur Levitt, former SEC commissioner, wrote an article on this topic in the *Wall Street Journal* dated October 21, 1999, titled "Point of View: Analysis through Rose-Colored Glasses." Here are a few points from that article:

Analysts often rely too heavily on guidance from companies, as opposed to doing their own research. Levitt expressed concern about investment banking firms pressuring their research analysts not to say things that could scare away current or potential corporate finance clients.

Levitt said that in some ways research departments have actually become marketing tools for Wall Street firms.

Levitt quoted from a memo that made the rounds through the corporate finance department at a prominent Wall Street firm: "We do not make negative or controversial comments about our clients as a matter of sound business practice... the philosophy and practical result needs to be no negative comments about our clients."

He said of the 27,000 or so individual analyst recommendations, only 270 are a "sell" or a "strong sell." In other words, about 99 percent of the ratings are "hold," "buy," or "strong buy." Levitt says something is wrong with those numbers. Can it be true that only 1 percent of the companies followed by major Wall Street analysts are investments that should be avoided?

What Should You Do Instead?

If you're reading this book, chances are you're either close to retirement or already retired. You may very well have a long history of successful investment. But you're probably wondering, given your changing circumstances, "Is it even possible at this critical juncture in my life to invest money in the stock market, make a profit, and limit my losses?" The answer is yes. In fact, the entire investment strategy of my practice has been built on the idea of making clients money, earning them a decent rate of return, but still protecting their assets from significant loss. We succeed in this endeavor by constantly weighing risk versus profit.

Now, I'm not saying that I can guarantee you'll maximize the profit potential of the stock market in a bull market and still guard against major loss. If that was possible, everyone would be a stock market millionaire. But we can avoid situations in which ill-prepared investors lose 20 percent, 30 percent, sometimes even 50 percent of their net worth seemingly overnight. That kind of loss is unacceptable and wholly avoidable.

In 2007, a man, whom I'll call Gary, and his wife came into my office looking for portfolio advice. He had just retired from Nortel, the multi-billion-dollar telecommunications giant. As part of his retirement package, Gary received two pensions, a basic pension and what was called an executive pension.

As soon as he sat down in my office, Gary said, "Look, I don't need much help; I'm just curious to see my options. I have more money coming between my pensions and social security than I can spend on a monthly basis. The 401(k) is really unnecessary."

I congratulated him on his massive success. There weren't many with such secure retirement prospects, I told him. Still, I said, he needed to have good risk management even on the money invested in his 401(k). You never know what can happen.

In fact, neither of us knew what was about to happen—the Great Recession of 2008. Among the many big company casualties of that era, Nortel filed for bankruptcy. Just like that, Gary had lost his executive pension.

When he next visited my office, Gary was a different man. His 401(k) was now his top priority. Without his executive pension, he and his wife wouldn't have enough in monthly income to sustain their standard of living.

"I need that money from my 401(k) now," Gary said. "What's it looking like?"

To his surprise and relief, I told Gary that his 401(k) was protected. All of his money was intact. In fact, for as long as the market stayed down between 2008 and 2010, Gary didn't sustain any meaningful losses. He was completely fine.

To this day, I still work with Gary, and every once in a while, he thanks me for what my office did for his family back in 2008. "I am so happy," he says, "that I had good risk management in place so that I didn't have to change my retirement plan."

Now don't misinterpret the point of that story. I am not claiming to have timed the market. I didn't magically foresee the events of 2008 and pull this gentleman's assets from the stock market just in time. The fact is no one really predicted what would happen in 2008. While some subscribe to the notion of market timing, the overwhelming majority of finance experts will tell you that a successful market timing strategy is a flying pig—it doesn't exist. I can say from my decades of experience in financial services, I have never seen a dependable market-timing approach. Instead, I believe in sell-side discipline. That means I buy when I see demand, but when demand diminishes, I sell—irrespective of market conditions.

Why do I believe in having a sell-side discipline in addition to a buy-side approach? Because 17 bear markets since 1929 support it. Applying both disciplines will provide the best protection of your principal while still allowing for growth. This balanced approach is process-based and completely independent from investment banking bias. It is emotionless risk management that is not based on storytelling or hidden agendas.

To prepare for changes in temperature, we may watch the thermometer. But watching the *barometer* vastly improves our understanding of the weather conditions beyond mere temperature readings. With investing, a thermometer is like *technical analysis*, and a barometer is like *fundamental analysis*. A thermometer shows conditions now, while a barometer indicates future conditions. As a barometer gives better insight into changing weather conditions, technical analysis gives better insight into the ever-changing conditions of the stock market and helps us navigate through them.

How does technical analysis help us?

Those who cannot remember the past are condemned to repeat it.

- George Santayana

First, it helps us determine the most attractive areas of the market by focusing on the strongest groups. Swimming with the tide makes the job of increasing or protecting wealth easier.

Second, technical analysis can help guide us to new opportunities while helping to steer us away from danger.

How do we apply technical analysis?

One handy mechanism we can use to apply what we learn through technical analysis is the **stop loss**. As the name of this investing technique implies, it is designed to protect our portfolios from steep losses that could otherwise take us by surprise. Investments like stocks and exchange-traded funds (ETFs) trade all day long on exchanges such as the New York Stock

Exchange. Stop losses are set to sell automatically when the stock price drops below a preset point.

Although past performance cannot guarantee future results, investment advisors may be able to help protect you from the full brunt of a major downturn using tools that can help identify current trends. If a major downturn doesn't happen overnight, they may be able to use other tools to reduce your exposure ahead of time. Remember, the return *of* your principal, especially when you are approaching retirement, is more important than the return *on* your principal.

When it comes to advising clients on what to do with their assets, I believe one of the key responsibilities that has been rudely ignored and sadly overlooked, particularly in bear markets, is the role of risk management. I believe the primary role of any financial advisor for his or her clients, especially when they reach that point in their lives when they are getting ready to switch gears from accumulation to distribution, is to be a competent, objective, and watchful risk manager.

Trailing Stop Losses

A *trailing stop loss* is a complex stop-loss order in which the stop is set at some fixed percentage below the market price. If the market price rises, the stop loss price rises proportionately, but if the stock price falls, the stop loss price doesn't change.

This technique allows us to set a limit on the maximum possible loss without setting a limit on the maximum possible gain. A trailing stop helps preserve profits while providing downside management.

Example: XYZ is purchased for $55 per share. Stop loss is set at $51.15.

The Process for Effective Risk Management

Anyone who understands weather patterns knows they are cyclical in nature. Because of the earth's rotation on its axis every 24 hours, because of its revolution around the sun every 365 days, and because of the natural forces of wind and temperature, it will be hot in the summer and cold in the winter, etc. Those facts are as plain as, well, day and night!

There are certain key elements to effective risk management that are as integral to that process as those natural forces just described:

First of all, effective risk managers do not ignore history. In fact, they embrace it as a predictor of what is going to happen again. For example, they remember that there have been 17 bear markets in the last 90 years! When one happens again, they will have a plan in place to protect your portfolio.

Second, they maintain a sell-side discipline. The best risk managers use a process-based system to help reduce the risk of large losses. They are removed from investment banking bias. They do not let income tax avoidance dictate risk management techniques or allow it to override their goals for principal preservation.

Third, savvy risk managers capitalize on the advantages of including technical analysis within their investment strategies, making emotionless investment decisions supported by current trends. They may use elements of fundamental analysis, but they do not base their risk management decisions solely on the stories told by the companies. Sound advisors depend more on the numbers because numbers don't lie.

Summary

Benjamin Graham, a famous economist, once said, "The essence of investment management is the management of risk, not the management of returns." That fact has not changed in the nearly 50 years since Graham died. To invest successfully, you must learn to identify and guard against risk first; then you can be confident in where you put your money. There will always be hot stock market options with promises of instant wealth. Don't succumb to alluring investments and neglect to assess their risk. According to Warren

Buffett, "The stock market is a device for transferring money from the impatient to the patient."

The cornerstone of my risk management approach is combining fundamental and technical analysis. Fundamental research tells us what ought to happen, while technical research tells us what is happening. These two methods, when combined, help us determine (a) which long-term investments are sound and (b) when they should be considered for purchase or sale.

We live in interesting financial times that offer up some unique opportunities to investors. Difficult markets force you to re-evaluate your strategies and views on risk and the effective management of risk. Now may be the time to refine your investment objective.

A competent financial advisor is someone who has thoroughly studied the terrain of your financial journey and is capable of explaining in detail the hazards, pitfalls, and dangers that lie ahead. It's your money. Don't be shy about asking the what-if questions. If your financial advisor hesitates, hems and haws, or otherwise fails to provide you with the details you need to proceed, I am going to go out on a limb here and suggest that you may need to look for another one.

CHAPTER 2

A Lifetime of Security—
Thanks to Lifetime Income

I had heard for a number of years that people fear out-living their money more than they fear death, but I always wondered if it was true. I had never seen any statistical proof of that assertion until the Allianz Life Insurance Company of North America conducted a survey in May 2010 and discovered that, sure enough, 61 percent of Americans between the ages of 44 and 75 feared running out of money in their old age more than they feared the grim reaper. The pollsters declared that there was a 2 percent margin of error, so it must be true. Since 2010, many research organizations have conducted similar experiments looking to verify or dis-prove the former results. They all found exactly the same thing.

When you think about it, however, that phobia is perfectly understandable. No one wants to die, but it has been statistically proven that eventually everybody will. Apparently, country music legend Hank Williams was right when he sang the lyrics to his 1952 hit, "I'll Never Get Out of This World Alive." The fear of outliving one's money is not just about the money. The fate that people fear more than death is losing their independence and becoming either a burden on their families or an indigent ward of the state.

The Allianz pollsters also found that about one-third of the 3,257 people surveyed knew very little about the mechanics of retirement, and they knew even less about such things as how much money they would need to pay their bills or where that money would come from.

"How much yearly income will you need in retirement?" When Allianz asked that question, the average response was $59,000 per year. "How much will you have to save to create that kind of income?" Most had no clue. Some took a stab at it, but they were way off—on the low side.

Baby Boomers' Savings Shortfall

Officially, a *baby boomer* is someone born between 1946 and 1964—so-called because of the sharp increase in the birth rate (baby boom) during those years. It began with soldiers returning home from World War

II to start families and plug into the great American dream.

Much has been written about the overwhelming economic and social impact of the baby boom generation. When they were infants, they began driving the economy. Everyone has heard of disposable diapers; baby boomers led to their invention as sure as the space race led to the invention of Velcro®. Bigger families needed bigger cars and more highways. Cities began sprawling into suburbs. The GI Bill made housing so affordable (you could buy a three-bedroom house for $5,000) that neighborhoods were being mass-produced like automobiles on an assembly line. And speaking of cars, you could get a new one for around $500. Television became part of American culture, and supermarkets were born. The economy was booming along with the birth rate.

As hard as it may be to comprehend, since 2011, these baby boomers have been retiring at a rate of 10,000 per day. It has been described as a "retirement tsunami." Believe it or not, the generation that gave us rock and roll music and put a man on the moon is now signing up for Social Security and Medicare!

Boomers were very good at making and spending money, but when it came to saving it...(finger waggle)...not so hot. According to the Allianz poll, 56 percent said they didn't think they would be able to cover their basic living expenses in retirement. Yet despite their fears, a majority of respondents among all age groups (79 percent) said they believe their retirement lifestyles should surpass those of their parents. I suppose it is fitting that the generation that developed instant coffee and invented the push-button world also came up with the idea for the credit card. Plastic-enabled boomers wanted all that the American cornucopia had to offer; they wanted it right away and had no idea how they were going to pay for it.

So it is safe to say that many boomers, especially those who came along later, are ill-prepared for retirement. Beyond having spent too much and saved too little, boomers will, on average, inherit less money than their parents did. Pensions are phasing out, and those who were depending on their 401(k) accounts had most of those assets invested in mutual funds. Mutual funds took a severe hit in the 2008 market crash. Most of them recovered within about ten years of the Great Recession. As I write this updated edition, however, mutual funds are down about 40 percent as a result of the coronavirus pandemic. Suffice it to say, as a class, boomers have some work to do on their plans for retirement, and the "my-dog-ate-my-homework" excuse won't wash this time around, Beaver Cleaver.

Life Expectancy and Retirement

It is a fact that people are living longer these days. According to data compiled by the Social Security Administration:

- A man reaching age 65 today can expect to live, on average, until age 84.

- A woman turning age 65 today can expect to live, on average, until age 86.

Keep in mind, those are just averages. About one out of every four 65-year-olds today will live past age 90, and one out of ten will live past age 95. Life expectancy tables are a little quirky in this respect: the longer you have lived, the longer they figure you will live. In other words, if you make it to 65, then there is a good chance you will live into your mid-80s. If you make it to 75, then your chances of living to age 90 are improved.

In doing the research for this book, I was surprised to learn that in 1900, the average male life expectancy was only 46 years of age! That means a 40-year-old would have been considered old by any measuring stick. And what do they say today? Sixty is the new 40? Today, someone in their 40s is considered to be in the prime of life.

By the time Social Security was introduced in 1936, the average life expectancy had increased to age 63. Today, a married couple aged 65 has a 40 percent probability for one of them to live to age 95. It is not uncommon for retirements today to last 30, even 40 years. As retirements grow longer, one of the great challenges retirees face is making their income last as long as they do. Because we are living longer, some folks will face a harsh reality.

Imagine you are retired and have lived much longer than you ever thought you would. Prices for everything have gone up. You try to hold the line on spending, but you can only do so much. It pains you to think of dipping into the remaining portion of your investments. That is your security. But you are beginning to think you have no alternative.

Yes, retirement income planning would be a lot easier if we only knew how long we would live. It would be simple math to take the available assets and stretch them out for a finite period. For most of us, however, that isn't possible. Lifespan is X, the unknown.

Once upon a time, between Social Security income from the government and corporate pension income from employers, people had as much as two-thirds of their retirement income *guaranteed*. Not now. Even the future of Social Security, which was once thought to be a permanent fixture of the retirement landscape, is now in question. The Social Security Administration (SSA) itself acknowledges that unless changes are made, the system may not be around for future generations. The chief actuary of the SSA has this disclaimer stamped at the top of the organization's website under the heading "The Future Financial Status of the Social Security Program":

> The concepts of solvency, sustainability, and budget impact are common in discussions of Social Security, but are not well understood. Currently, the Social Security Board of Trustees projects program cost to rise by 2035 so that taxes will be enough to pay for only 75 percent of scheduled benefits.

He concludes a few sentences later that without reform "benefits will necessarily be lowered with no effect on budget deficits."

What about retirement income from corporations? Most corporations have discontinued pension plans. The defined *benefit* pension plans have been replaced with defined *contribution* retirement savings plans. This means the responsibility has been shifted; it is now up to the employee to save for his or her retirement. The company may or may not match what you contribute to the plan up to a percentage of your income. What is the result for our baby boomers? Now, only approximately one-third—just the part from Social Security—of their retirement income is guaranteed.

Cycle of Emotions for Individual Investors

When individuals assume the responsibility for forging their own retirement programs and take on the role of professional investors, things don't always turn out so well. Ask anyone what the goal of investing should be, and they will say, "Buy low and sell high," and maybe add "obviously." But there is another element individual investors have to deal with that gets in the way—human emotions. This is especially true of those investing with retirement in view. The larger retirement looms in our time window, the more heightened our emotions become. We feel pressured to stay invested no matter what happens in the market. Fears of outliving our income kick in when there is a market downturn, and we start entertaining the idea of doubling down, as they say in Las Vegas—that is, taking on more risk in an effort to make up for lost time. When markets fluctuate and our emotions, fears, and concerns naturally surface, we end up doing the exact opposite of buying low and selling high.

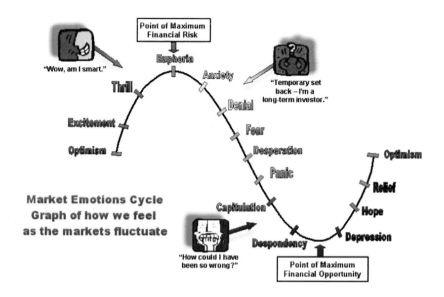

Point of Maximum
Financial Risk

Euphoria

"Wow, am I smart."

Anxiety

Thrill

"Temporary set
back – I'm a
long-term investor."

Denial

Excitement

Fear

Optimism

Desperation

Optimism

Panic

Relief

**Market Emotions Cycle
Graph of how we feel
as the markets fluctuate**

Capitulation

Hope

Despondency

Depression

"How could I have
been so wrong?"

Point of Maximum
Financial Opportunity

The cycle of emotions we may feel in a volatile market:

OPTIMISM—The cycle starts with a positive feeling we have about a particular investment. We buy the stock feeling confident that our risk is warranted since we believe this stock will do well and we will be rewarded.

EXCITEMENT—The stock moves up, and we begin to get excited. We anticipate the future, thinking of how this story will play out when we are able to tell our fellow investors what a good trade we made.

THRILL—This is even better! The stock continues to move up without a hitch. We can't help but feel at this point that we are pretty darn smart. Our trading system rocks!

EUPHORIA—Hey! No risk, no reward, right? We are on a roll! This is the point of our maximum financial risk, but it is also the point of maximum financial reward. Greed takes over. We pour even more money into this stock and wish we had done it earlier—this dude is a winner!

ANXIETY—Oh no, it's…it's…it's starting to go the other way! Just when we invested more than we told ourselves we would, the market is turning around. It is beginning to turn our hard-won gains into small losses. But only a fool would get out now. We have too much in this thing. If you can't take the heat, then get out of the kitchen! We're in this for the long haul; we can take the heat. We still think the long-term trend is going to be higher.

DENIAL—Okay, so the market didn't behave exactly as we had hoped. That still doesn't mean our trading skills are off. These things happen sometimes. It will turn around. This is just normal stock market jitters. We will be fine.

FEAR—This is where reality sets in. Maybe we're not as smart as we thought we were. Confidence is replaced by confusion. We see our losses coming back to haunt us in the form of real pain and sacrifice. Our self-talk starts to sound something like: "Don't be a fool. Sure, you've lost almost all of your gains, but if you get out now with just a little profit, you'll live to trade another day." But we can't pull the sell trigger for some reason. We wait another day. It would be a shame to pull out just when the market is starting to turn back around.

DESPERATION—Now all the gains are gone. We had a chance to make a profit and missed it. We have to act now to get back in the black, but red ink is gushing. This is not good!

PANIC—We feel helpless at the mercy of this vicious and cruel market. Now at the most emotional point of this entire episode, we feel clueless and out of control. If we had only known this was going to happen.

CAPITULATION—Get out! Get out now! They have broken us. We can stand no more losses. All we want to do now is sell, sell, sell...salvage what we can. The only smart thing to do is get out and avoid any more losses.

DESPONDENCY—Our self-talk at this point goes something like: "Never again! I will never buy stocks again, ever! The stock market is not for people like me. I will avoid it like the plague from now on. It's a sucker's game." Interestingly, although we are not aware of it, this is our point of greatest financial opportunity.

DEPRESSION—Now, we're saying, "Bartender, make mine a double. How could I have been so stupid?" We walk around like our favorite sports team just lost a big game, we wrecked the car, and our dog died—all on the same day.

HOPE—As time passes, we see the market curve upward again. It was just a glitch, after all. If we stayed in, we could have broken even. If we only had the foresight, we could have recognized that the bottom is the time to buy. We can still do this! Hey, there is an opportunity here after all! We start analyzing the market for new investment opportunities.

RELIEF—The markets are turning back into positive territory again. The investment that turned so sour on us is beginning to come back around as well. Our faith in the market and our ability to invest money is restored. Invest again—that's the ticket! (And the cycle starts all over again.)

The above cycle explains why the average investor earns less than actual market returns. Researchers have published several studies that prove this point statistically. According to DALBAR, the financial services industry's leading research organization, over the 20-year period that ended in 2011, the average investor earned 2.1 percent—not even keeping up with inflation, which ran 2.5 percent over the same period. That's what chasing performance and trying to time the market will do for you.

The Need for a Structured Plan

More than ever before, we need a structured income plan—one that eliminates guesswork—to provide us with security in retirement. An effective structured income plan should ensure that we will be able to enjoy retirement without worrying whether we will prematurely exhaust our resources or have to drastically adjust our lifestyles.

One thing I have noticed about the baby boomers, at least those who have sought my opinions lately, is that the word *guarantee* seems to be important to them. They seem to much prefer the word *guarantee* over the word *projection* when it comes to income in retirement. That's entirely understandable after the last Wall Street debacle. We are much better off knowing what *will* happen than what *might* happen.

When it comes to creating an effective income plan, you can find about as many approaches as there are financial advisors. But not all of the resulting income plans (a) account for and adjust for inflation and (b) are guaranteed to last for the rest of your life. Many investors focus on ROI, or return on investment. I propose a new definition of ROI: **reliability of income**. The approach I recommend focuses on the amount of time you can be in the market to ensure you end up with reliable, inflation-adjusted income for retirement.

Structured Income Plan Framework

To start, let's take a 25-year period and divide it into five equal segments, each segment representing five years. Our investments in these five segments will range from conservative to aggressive. Now, let's add a sixth segment representing the period beyond 25 years. The more aggressive investments will be held in the segments that allow for the longest time periods in the market. Research has indicated that the risk of volatility increases as investment classes become more aggressive, but that risk is mitigated over time. The time factor enables us to realize the higher rates of return that have been historically associated with more aggressive investments. Of course, most of us are familiar with the commonly used disclaimer: "Past performance is not a guarantee of future results."

Roger G. Ibbotson is a professor of finance at the Yale School of Management who has written extensively on capital market returns, cost of capital, and international investment. In one project, Ibbotson measured actual investment class performance over a 50-year period, segmented just like the example I set up for us. In Ibbotson's project, the shorter the time frame, the more conservative the income-producing investments. What were his findings?

- **Segment one** (years 1–5): One-year Treasury bills averaged 5.3 percent.*

- **Segment two** (years 6–10): Intermediate government bonds held for 5-year periods averaged 7.26 percent.*

- **Segment three** (years 11–15): The S&P 500 Composite Stock Index held for 10-year periods averaged 10.58 percent.*

- **Segment four** (years 16–20): Large-cap stocks held for 15-year periods averaged 11.18 percent.*

- **Segment five** (years 21–25): Small-cap stocks held for 20-year periods averaged 14.78 percent.*

- **Segment six** (year 26 and beyond): Small-cap stocks held for 25-year periods averaged 14.91 percent.*

These are historical rates of return and do not include any investment expenses or fees. To account for today's current economic climate, rates of return will be reduced considerably for examples or illustrations in this book.

To continue building our example, we will need to make some assumptions. Keep in mind we are doing this with the goal of producing reliable income for retirement. We could put any number of investments into this matrix, but here are some suggestions based on my experience.

- **Segment one:** Immediate income annuities, laddered CD portfolios, and other fixed-income vehicles. The key for this segment is to provide guaranteed monthly income.

- **Segment two:** Short-term bonds and fixed annuity contracts.

- **Segment three:** Investments subject to stock market risk.

- **Segments four, five, and six:** Investment vehicles offering more aggressive growth portfolios.

Probably one of the most crucial steps in creating a structured income plan is identifying your income needs. At every educational seminar I teach, someone asks, "What's the magic number?" That is, how much money do you need to have saved to retire with confidence? Normally, they assume it's $1 million. I don't know who started the insidious rumor that $1 million is the cover-all retirement nest egg finish line, but I'd like to have a few words with him.

The fact is that "magic number" will be different for each of us. You don't have to nail this number down to the penny, but your planner should be able to help you arrive at a number that accurately reflects how much you will need each month to pay your bills and cover your necessary expenses. Let's call this your "income for needs"—the "floor" for your absolute basic requirements. The wellspring for this income should be kept safe. You want this money to get a good rate of return if possible, but losing any of it is just not an option. For your income needs, rate of return is not a priority; safety of principal is.

Below are the three essential categories of income that will compose our structured income plan:

1. **Income for needs**—Most of these items will be self-evident—things you need on an annual or monthly basis—like food, clothing, insurance, mortgage/rent, property taxes, and utilities. Can you think of any others? This category is for what I call "non-negotiable expenses"—things you can't live without. The income floor is the minimum amount you will need each month throughout your entire retirement.

2. **Income for wants**—This is the fun category. What do you want to buy? What do you want to do? Where do you want to go? Be reasonable, but if you want it, put it here. Vacations? A new car? Home upgrades, like new carpet, for example? Maybe you would like to pamper yourself with an occasional spa treatment? Or perhaps you enjoy dining out from time to time? You may not need these things to live, but they will make your life more enjoyable. When estimating wants, consider the different phases of retirement. In early retirement, you may be more active and have a greater desire to travel, for example, than when you are older. Will your wants be the same in year 15 of your retirement as they were in year one? Probably not.

3. **Income for gifting**—If you are able to do so, helping others when you retire is a great source of satisfaction. This may include helping your grandchildren with college. Some retirees like to donate to their favorite charities. I have some clients who tell me they want to help their children now, instead of having them wait for inheritance. I understand that. That way, the giver is able to enjoy the smiles on the faces of those who benefit from their gifts. Obviously, your plans for this category are personal, and the choices are yours.

Structured Income Plan Illustration

Now that I've laid out the framework for the plan, let's add some details to bring the full structured income plan illustration to life.

John and Mary are excited! They are six months away from the day they have looked forward to for years—their retirement! They have thought through the three categories of income listed above—needs, wants, and gifts—and arrived at some conclusions.

Their income needs are $3,800 per month. Their income wants come out to $15,000 per year, or $1,250 per month. John and Mary have two grandchildren, and since their children are well taken care of by their own successful careers, the couple would like to put

$500 per month toward their grandchildren's college education—gifting income. The total income needed to meet the goals of all three categories comes to $5,500 per month. That doesn't include the taxes that must be paid, so when we figure income taxes on top of that (assuming a 25 percent tax bracket), that brings the gross total income requirement to $6,938 per month.

Sources of income

Where is the money coming from to fund these three categories? John and Mary have assets from (a) retirement accounts, (b) savings, and (c) fixed-income sources:

Invested Assets	
John's 401(k)	$525,000
Mary's 401(k)	$240,000
Roth IRAs combined	$62,000
Brokerage account	$250,000
Savings in CDs/money markets	$70,000
Total invested assets	**$1,147,000**
Fixed Income	
John's Social Security	$1,500/month
Mary's Social Security	$1,000/month
Mary's pension	$1,000/month
Total fixed income	**$3,500/month**

We now know John and Mary's future income needs, wants, and gifts, as well as their current assets and fixed income. Remember, for their income needs, John and Mary need a net income of $3,800 per month. If we gross up this amount for income tax, then they will need about $4,750 per month. This means they need an additional $1,250 per month ($4,750 needed −$3,500 fixed income = $1,250), just to cover their needs.

There are key points to consider when choosing the type of financial vehicle to produce the $1,250 per month:

- The amount of income should be guaranteed.
- The income should not be determined based on the rate of return of the underlying investment.
- The length of time the financial vehicle produces the income should cover the couple's lifetime.

Will John and Mary need some financial planning assistance at this point? Absolutely! They have been good savers and good "accumulators" for their retirement, but they are finished with the accumulation phase of their financial lives. Now, they are about to enter the distribution phase, when their assets must begin replacing the paychecks they will be leaving behind.

Of course, they want to keep their accumulated assets working for them throughout their retirement years, but it is imperative to keep their assets, period! That is why I recommend contacting a financial planner who specializes in retirement income planning.

A Word on Inflation

To avoid overcomplicating John and Mary's example, let's look at another couple, Robert and Becky, to make a quick point about inflation. We'll come back to John and Mary later.

Robert and Becky read this chapter on retirement income just like you're reading it now, and they decided it'd be worth sitting down with a financial professional. So they visited my office.

When I first met Robert and Becky, they were both aged 60. Their goal was to retire at 65. Like most soon-to-be retirees, their primary concern was "Do we have enough to retire?" More than anything, they wanted me to give them that ever-elusive magic number.

Instead, I asked, "What are your essential income needs?" In other words, how much do you need to keep the lights on, to keep the house paid for, to buy food, to afford health care expenses? Then I asked them about their wants. Finally, I asked if they planned to gift any of their money. Does all this sound familiar yet?

Robert and Becky told me they weren't interested in gifting anything. So that left needs and wants. After some number crunching and budget making, we came to $4,500 a month in essential income. To satisfy their wants, they'd need another $2,000. That makes for $6,500 total, easy math. But here's the tricky part— my point in including this brief side example—Robert and Becky were still five years from retirement. When we tabulated all their expenses and came to $6,500 in monthly income, Robert and Becky were ready to go home. That's what they'd been looking for: they just had to multiply $6,500 by the number of months they expected to live in retirement, and they'd land upon the magic number, right?

Wrong!

They forgot about inflation. Over the last 100 years, the average yearly inflation has been about 3 percent. Assuming 3 percent each year over the five years before Robert and Becky could retire *inflated* their monthly income from $6,500 to $7,535. You read that right, over $1,000 in just five years.

Imagine what could have happened if Robert and Becky had gone about the last few years of their working lives blissfully planning to save for $6,500 a month. In their very first month of retired life, they would have realized they were $1,000 over budget. Just thinking about that situation gives me stress. What's more, $7,535 wouldn't remain their monthly income need throughout retirement either—eventually, it would creep up to $8,000 and beyond.

Inflation is a scary thing. For the purposes of this example, we assumed a constant 3 percent rate, but that's not how things work in the real world. Some well-meaning financial professionals have developed sweeping rules in an effort to simplify the retirement process for the average investor. For example, you may have heard of the 4 percent rule—withdraw no more than 4 percent of your assets each year, and you should never run out of money. Great, if only it worked that easily.

In reality, there is no simple formula or plan that fits every investor and always works. There are too many shifting variables; circumstances vary too widely. When I sit down with potential clients to assess their financial standing and retirement needs, it's not as simple as estimating average potential inflation over the next few decades and assuming their circumstances will stay fairly constant. I use sophisticated software that can run hundreds of manipulations to ensure that a client's portfolio is keeping them on track for success regardless of unexpected changes. What if someone needs long-term health care eventually? What if they need extra insurance? What if one spouse predeceases the other? What if they want to buy a second home? What if they want to remodel their current home? Such questions and any others you can imagine are accounted for in our software.

Professional Help to Inspire Confidence

If you're at all thinking to yourself, "These simplified examples still seem kind of complicated," don't feel bad. I'm throwing a lot of numbers at you all at once. The fact is retirement planning isn't simple. Some investment products are marketed as the end-all, be-all to meet all your retirement needs. That's a gimmick. To develop a robust retirement income plan takes some effort. That's where a financial professional can make a big difference. Let me illustrate it this way: When seeking medical attention, we see a specialist with training and expertise specific to our current ailment. As children, we saw pediatricians; as adults, we see either a general practitioner or a specialist, depending on our needs. For a heart problem, we see a cardiologist. For a toothache, we see a dentist. Retirement income planning warrants the same level of expertise.

One regrettable difference between the medical profession and the financial advisory profession is that doctors will usually tell you if the condition you are bringing to them is outside their scope of training. You can't always count on that from every financial advisor. This doesn't necessarily mean anyone is intentionally trying to mislead you. Some advisors simply may not be aware that they are not qualified to offer the specific kind of advice you need.

Just as there are various philosophies in the medical field that can steer diagnosis and treatment, there are various investing philosophies in the financial advisory community. Some financial professionals are trained to believe the solution to every planning problem lies solely in equities; others are trained to believe it lies solely in fixed annuities. There is an old proverb that says, "It is tempting, if the only tool you have is a hammer, to treat everything as if it were a nail." Professionals who are trained in nothing but equities and the stock market tend to exemplify that adage. Professionals whose view is limited to just insurance products tend to wear blinders to the benefits of equities, and so forth. Retirement income specialists, however, must be acquainted with all features and facets of the financial landscape and have a working knowledge of all the latest tools, strategies, and concepts available.

Is it possible for a blend of the equity and fixed-annuity approaches to be the most effective strategy for a structured retirement income plan? Consider another medical analogy: I know a friend who was diagnosed with a type of lymphoma. The oncologists recommended chemotherapy. A doctor who specializes in natural cures recommended that she restrict her diet to organic raw vegetables, take lots of supplements, and submit to pH (potential hydrogen) therapy. She implemented both doctors' recommendations. Within six months she was happy to report a clean PET (positron emission tomography) scan. It has been five years, and there's still no recurrence of the cancer. Naturally, both doctors claim it was their treatment plan that got rid of the cancer and the other was a waste of time. My friend is just happy to be feeling better.

Bottom line, I recommend working with a financial planner who (a) specializes in retirement planning and (b) works on a fiduciary basis. A retirement planning specialist will be able to bring a number of financial products to the table to solve the problem. A retirement planning specialist will have macroscopic—not microscopic—vision. That is, they will see the entire picture. A fiduciary is a financial professional who is under legal and ethical obligation to advise you irrespective of any fees, commissions, or other remunerations he or she may receive. He or she has sworn to place your interests ahead of his or her own. (See chapter 7 for further explanation.)

Going back to our illustration, one option that could work for John and Mary is an annuity with an attached rider that guarantees an income stream for life. In the world of annuities, there are many options. We'll cover these thoroughly in chapter 5, but I'll give you some of the highlights now.

Earlier I mentioned that retirees love to find "guaranteed" income. I'm sure that sounds appealing to you too. Annuities can be one of the few options that genuinely come with a guarantee. But not all annuities are created equal.

If you're going to get an annuity, you probably want a deferred annuity. These come with a guarantee of future income, *future* being the operative word. You'll contribute money to the annuity under the condition that you wait a certain amount of time before tapping into the income, hence deferring it.

Deferred annuities include several different types. One is called a variable annuity. Under almost every circumstance, I do not recommend investing your hard-earned money in a variable annuity. It's not guaranteed. The eventual income is still deferred, but the principal you contribute is invested in the stock market via mutual funds where it's subject to regular market fluctuation and loss. And that's not to mention the exorbitant fees that come with variable annuities.

On the other hand, fixed annuities can be an excellent contribution to your investment portfolio. With these, your principal is protected. The only way your principal will go down is if you withdraw the money yourself. Fixed annuities can be further divided into traditional fixed annuities and fixed index annuities (FIAs). Both can serve you well, but FIAs are especially capable investment vehicles. Your contributed money is invested in the stock market but still with the guarantee that you will never lose your principal. Your interest is linked to an index (hence the name), which could be something like the S&P 500, the NASDAQ, or the Dow Jones. As the market trends upward, you will likewise see rising interest on your money. If the market bottoms out, however, your annuity is floored at zero percent. That means while you may not make any money for a time, neither will you lose any. Thus, FIAs offer very low volatility with a high potential earning capacity.

You must be careful to fully consider fees and terms before signing any annuity contract, but the advantage of an annuity is that it can be a source of *guaranteed income* (subject to the financial strength and claims-paying ability of the issuing insurance company). It would be advisable to consult a fee-based financial advisor who can give you unbiased information about the pros and cons of the annuities you are considering. Some annuities can have high fees and surrender charges, and you must watch out for those. But some insurance companies today have created annuities with much lower fees and no surrender charges.

In a free-market society like ours, companies are constantly changing their product offerings to remain competitive in the marketplace. That's why American automobile manufacturers completely retooled and reinvented themselves when buyers began to favor the sleeker, more fuel-efficient cars made in Japan. Insurance companies are profit-driven companies too. Their annuity offerings were bland and staid back in the 1980s and early 1990s. Let's put it this way: Fixed annuities weren't exactly flying off the shelves, which is why a few of the larger insurance companies completely retooled these financial instruments in the early 2000s to include a variety of welcome changes. Smaller companies eventually followed suit, and many of these new annuity designs now satisfy the one major itch that baby boomers seem to want scratched—guaranteed lifetime income. You will want to do thorough research before purchasing an annuity to make sure it is acceptable and suitable for your situation, but some of the new varieties can be quite useful in certain retirement income plans.

Let's revisit our example of John and Mary. What if they could find an annuity that would guarantee to pay out 5.5 percent of the balance for the rest of their lives? In order for them to receive the $1,250 per month to fulfill their income floor, they would need to place approximately $272,728 in the annuity. This investment would guarantee them $15,000 per year, or $1,250 per month (5.5 percent of $272,728). (Please keep in mind, this example is not product specific or company specific and may not be a good choice for your particular situation.) A rider on the annuity contract could allow for a specific percentage of the balance to be paid as *income for life*, regardless of the performance of the initial amount put into the annuity.

Once John and Mary have chosen a financial vehicle to provide the $1,250 per month, they can move on to considering how to fund the remaining segments of their structured income plan. As they do so, they can feel at ease knowing that their basic income needs are taken care of. This is a major step in achieving a worry-free retirement. Just think of what this step would have accomplished! Regardless of what the market does or does not do, and regardless of what prevailing rates of return happen to be, their basic income needs will be met. That income floor will not be affected because it is fixed. They can go to sleep each night without having to worry about waking up to news of a deteriorating economy. Now they have the freedom to focus on what they may feel are the more important things—the things in life not associated with finances.

Each of the segments in John and Mary's structured income plan has a job. Segments one, two, and three will provide additional income for their wants and gifting desires. When funding these segments, it is important to remember that the income desired is immediate. You would not want to take very high risks in these segments, because risky investments could erase principal due to a stock market decline.

Segments four through six will be invested for longer time horizons, with the goal of providing growth for future income needs and as a hedge against inflation. In these segments, there could be balance fluctuations from time to time. This should be no cause for alarm because the goals for these segments are different. You do not need immediate income from these segments. So if the market takes a dip, the anxiety you would have ordinarily felt will be greatly reduced. You will not worry about your income needs and feel forced to sell your investments at the wrong time. You will have more confidence about staying invested for the longer term. Studies have shown that, in most cases, the longer you stay invested, the greater chance you have to make a positive return. While no one likes to see their investment balances go down, you can look at these segments in a different light.

Most retirees correlate their investment balances to their income, but with this income plan, the two are not attached. Your income will continue, and your basic needs will be taken care of through your investments in segments one through three while your other investments fluctuate—hopefully growing over time—with the market.

The goal with this type of structured income plan is to allow you to get off the emotional roller coaster. I can remember, as a kid, looking forward with glee and excitement to riding roller coasters. The ones at the North Carolina State Fair were okay, but they weren't very scary because they had to be put up and taken down each year and were therefore limited in size. Then I met the big one—Thunder Road at Carowinds Amusement Park in Charlotte, North Carolina. I loved it. This giant wooden thrill ride was named after the 1958 movie *Thunder Road*, which featured moonshine-running hot rod cars. This explained why two mock moonshine stills were set up at the entrance to the ride. I think the set decorations were lost on most of the kids, who had probably never seen the movie. They were more interested in the ride's kinetic attributes. I can still remember the clackity-clack of the chain as it pulled the car up almost 100 feet and then dropped me and the other occupants in a virtual free fall. I don't know if they are still there or not, but there used to be a series of signs on the way up that read, "Grit your teeth...bear the load...enjoy your ride...on Thunder Road." These days I take my kids to amusement parks and *watch* as they ride roller coasters. Personally, I no longer have any desire to be slung around and tossed about. It is definitely something for the younger crowd.

Investing sentiments are quite similar. When we are young, both our portfolios and our emotions can take the up-and-down thrills of a volatile and unpredictable stock market. Market crash? No problem. We didn't have that much in it anyway, and besides, it will come back around eventually. And that's right! It does come back around, eventually. But as we age and near retirement, we find the thrill rides chilling and uncomfortable. Perhaps this is because we have a great deal more at stake than we did when we were youngsters. We also do not have time to wait for the market to rebound. In the past, some retirees may have kept their retirement accounts placed in risky investments because they knew of no other alternatives. Some still do that. As a consequence, when the market declines, they feel it is necessary to stop taking income. This restricts their lifestyle and adds to their anxiety.

The main advantage of a structured income plan is that it cannot be jeopardized by a decline in the stock market. A well-thought-out retirement plan is one of the best cures for insomnia among retirees. Just

imagine the peace of mind that can result fr\
ing you don't have to worry about your income.

In the past, most have labored under the mistaken notion that they must take extra risks or forfeit future growth. This is simply not necessary with a structured income plan. Why? Because while you have segments one through three providing income, you have segments four through six invested for future growth. You will also realize that you are achieving ROI as we have redefined it—reliability of income. With the first three segments, this reliability of income is more important in retirement years than the return on investment.

Plan Review

I have purposefully kept this discussion of structured income plans to a big-picture view. Each situation will vary. The specifics of your income plan will need to be tailored to fit your unique financial situation. I don't know of anyone who has the exact same income needs and identical assets.

It is important to monitor the plan closely. If you work with an advisor, this would be something you do together. I recommend getting at least a quarterly update with a more extensive annual review. I like to think of the client as the CEO (chief executive officer) of their retirement plan, and the advisor as the CFO (chief financial officer). This means you are the boss and you call the shots. The advisor implements and monitors the plan, reporting the results to you.

As the CEO, you have responsibilities. Make sure you completely understand the income plan and any investments your advisor recommends to you. Do your research and ask lots of questions. Your advisor should be patient and answer your questions in detail. You want to thoroughly understand exactly how your advisor will get paid and whether there are conflicts of interest with their recommendations. By creating a structured income plan and following this guidance, you can have peace of mind that is essential for a purposeful and fulfilling retirement.

CHAPTER 3

Tax-Reduction Strategies

As Jeff Foxworthy would say, "You might just be a baby boomer if...you know what a Studebaker was." For the rest of you, it was a car. In fact, at one point, Studebaker was the largest automobile manufacturer in the world.

One problem with the Studebaker, and perhaps the reason why it is now extinct, was that it was actually ahead of its time. The Studebaker Corporation, named for its wagon-maker founder, John M. Studebaker, entered the automotive business in 1902 with electric cars, introducing gasoline-powered models two years later.

Over time, the eponymous Studebaker sedan developed a reputation for being sleek, fast, and dependable. By the time the 1960s rolled around, however, the auto manufacturer was having trouble moving merchandise, and the last Studebaker rolled off the line on March 16, 1966.

What does all this have to do with individual retirement accounts? Quite a bit, actually. When Studebaker began closing down plants and sending workers home, they realized their pension plans were so poorly funded they could not afford to pay all their employees' pensions. As a result, thousands of workers either got nothing or had their payouts drastically reduced.

Those auto workers weren't about to take this lying down. They complained vociferously to Congress. The chorus was soon joined by other workers whose companies had defaulted on their pension commitments.

The hue and cry forced Congress to act. In 1974, the legislature enacted the Employee Retirement Income Security Act, often referred to as ERISA, to regulate pension plans. One of the by-products of ERISA was a new provision called the *individual retirement account,* or IRA.

The new law provided that a taxpayer could contribute up to $1,500 per year into an IRA and reduce his or her taxable income by the same amount. It was great for self-employed individuals, who had no pension plans. The tax-advantaged IRA also allowed the money in the account to grow tax-deferred. You didn't have to pay taxes on the money until you withdrew it.

What a sweet deal, right? Since no taxes were coming out as the account accrued interest, the compounding was accelerated. Your interest earned interest, and the interest on the interest earned interest.

Good old Uncle Sam! Of course, tax deferral—don't forget—is good for the government too. Tax-*deferred* is not tax-*free*. Uncle Sam will get his slice of a much bigger pie later on; meanwhile, he can print all the money he needs. But what if your employer offers a matching 401(k) plan? Well, there is no law against having both a 401(k) and an IRA.

To date, IRAs have become very popular. Millions of Americans have socked away trillions of dollars in them and seem to be cruising along just fine. I am not a pilot, but those I have talked to tell me that landing an airplane is the most difficult part of flying. The IRA is pretty straightforward during the *accumulation* phase. Owners are thrilled to see their tax bills decrease and their investment balances grow as they contribute pre-tax dollars to their IRAs. But when folks enter the *distribution* phase—otherwise known as retirement— they discover the IRA is perhaps a bit more complex than other savings and investment instruments.

Questions arise about preserving assets and making funds last. Even more questions arise about how to pass the inheritance along to heirs. I am reminded of those mazes in which white mice are timed to see how quickly they can find their way out. Unless you know how to maneuver through the maze of rules and regulations, you may feel as if you are encountering obstacles at every turn when it comes time to either withdraw funds from your IRA or pass them along to your heirs.

If you feel frustrated or confused, don't worry—you're not alone. Fortunately, there are solutions to the tax puzzle. You can minimize your taxes without subverting the law.

Tax Evasion Versus Tax Avoidance

Taxes are the law. They must be paid, one way or another. When I first became a financial advisor, a mentor told me this joke: "What's the difference between tax evasion and tax avoidance...?"

"Ten to 20 years."

I know it's a bit corny, but the point is sound. Investors should never withhold taxes owed to the government. But neither should they pay *more* than what they legally owe. In fact, the United States government has published a document that includes *thousands* of ways to avoid overpaying on your taxes. That's great! Right? Well, it would be great if it wasn't buried in the four million-word, 74,608-page Internal Revenue Service Tax Code.

In case those figures are not impressive enough, let's compare the IRS tax code to some better-known works of literature. Remember Leo Tolstoy's *War and Peace*, that formidable instrument of high school torture? That one clocks in at a meager 587,287 words—just a little over 1,200 pages. Almost twice that length is J. K. Rowling's popular Harry Potter series if we put all the books together. The Authorized King James Bible sits somewhere in the middle with 783,137 words. All three books together just barely exceed half the IRS tax code's length. It's probably not unreasonable to say that the average investor will never read the government's official tax code.

Even if you were to sit down and power through the document, you'd be hard-pressed to extract tax-saving tips in a comprehensive and, more importantly, practical way. You won't find convenient subheadings like "How to Avoid Overtaxation" or "Read This for the Bottom Line." Finding useful support in the millions of words is more akin to a treasure hunt—and you haven't been given the map.

The Internal Revenue Service itself admits that its tax code is too complicated. In 1913, the document was 400 pages long. In 1939, it jumped to 504. Then things started to go terribly wrong. By 1969, it had increased to 16,500 pages, 26,300 pages by 1984, 60,044 in 2004, and finally the 74,608 we've had since 2014. How could they possibly have had so much to add? In 2008, the Taxpayer Advocate Service's Annual Report to Congress from the IRS read in part: "The most serious problem facing taxpayers is the complexity of the Internal Revenue Code." Understatement of the year. And it didn't stop the IRS from adding another 14,564 pages six years later. *Forbes,* "Tax Code Hits Nearly 4 Million Words," January 10, 2013; *The Washington Post,* "Ted Cruz's claim that the IRS tax code has more words than the Bible," March 11, 2015; wordcounter.net; *The Washington Examiner,* "Look at How Many Pages Are in the Federal Tax Code," April 15, 2016; www.irs.gov/pub/tas/08_tas_arc_msp_1. pdf

I think Ed Slott, a leading IRA expert, said it best in his book, *The Retirement Savings Time Bomb...and How to Defuse It*: "Due to a complex combination of distribution and estate taxes that kick in at retirement or death, millions of you are at risk of losing much—perhaps even most—of your retirement savings."

The Basics of Tax Reduction

Even without understanding the ins and outs of the IRS Tax Code, some basic rules of thumb can tremendously reduce the amount of taxes you owe Uncle Sam. Most people will draw from a combination of various accounts to fund their retirement income. The taxes you will owe depend heavily on *how* you withdraw your money.

It's commonly recommended that retirees fund their retirement in a certain order of withdrawals. They should begin retirement pulling money (1) from taxable accounts. When those are expended, (2) start drawing from tax-deferred retirement accounts like IRAs and 401(k)s. Finally, (3) tap into accounts where taxes have already been paid. The most famous of those options is the Roth IRA.

For some retirees, this "withdrawal protocol" is the best course of action. But beware, one size *does not* fit all, and these times represent a different tax environment than previous decades. For example, you might have most of your savings in a 401(k) or a traditional IRA. Let's say you reach the required minimum distribution (RMD) zone at 72 years old. If you've accumulated a hefty sum in your 401(k), the RMD could be enough to catapult you into a higher tax bracket. (Even if it doesn't at first, wait until you're in your 80s when RMDs increase with decreased remaining life expectancy.) Suddenly, you're facing unexpectedly high taxes. To avoid those, it may be wise to adjust your withdrawal strategy. You could move some money from your 401(k) to a more tax-friendly account or use tax-deferred accounts as your first source of retirement income.

The example above is specific and may not describe your situation. The point is that every soon-to-be retiree needs to examine his or her circumstances individually. Every soon-to-be retiree must examine his or her current tax bracket environment relative to historical rates and current economic data. Taxes are likely to rise in the future, and tax strategies must account for that. It's also important to understand how retirement income is taxed in the first place. It comes down to the source. The following is not an exhaustive look at income sources and their tax setups, but it covers many of the most common options. I recommend always consulting a professional for an in-depth look at your specific situation—one with expertise in tax planning. Taxes make up a critical component of any retirement plan. If your financial advisor cannot assist with tax planning, you will miss a huge slice of the retirement planning pie.

- Tax-deferred accounts, which include 401(k)s, 403(b)s, 457s, Thrift Savings Plans (TSPs), traditional IRAs, and deferred annuities are taxed as ordinary income upon withdrawal. Interest on certificates of deposit (CDs), savings accounts, and money market accounts are likewise considered regular income.

- Interest received from municipal bonds is exempt from federal income tax. *However*, you must remember that municipal bonds may be subject to state and local taxes. Make sure you know what your state expects from you before pulling income from bonds.

- Profit from selling stocks, bonds, or mutual funds is taxed as capital gains. That means that the tax rate varies based on when you purchased the investment and how long you owned it. In general, it's best for the retiree to keep these investments for some time before selling. After a year, assets are taxed at long-term capital gains rates, which are generally more favorable than the alternative—short-term capital gains, which are taxed as ordinary income.

- If you have a Roth IRA, if you're older than 59½, and if you've owned the Roth IRA for at least five years, the money in that account is generally safe from the taxman. As an extra bonus, you're not required to withdraw a required minimum distribution at age 72. There's a lot more to Roth IRAs, so we'll look at them again later (in the chapter after next).

- If you have a pension, congratulations. You're one of few who still do. Typically, pensions are taxed as regular income, but that's not always the case. For example, if you've made after-tax contributions to your pension, it will probably be taxed differently. The only way to be sure is to examine your pension plan specifically.

- Annuities are a popular retirement income source, and there are several annuity types and tax setups. The rules depend on the annuity you own and the source of the purchase funds. As with pension plans, it's best to look at your specific annuities to see how they will be taxed. In general, however, annuities are divided into two tax groups: The part that represents the principal is tax-free. The growth is taxed as ordinary income.

- Social security may be taxed, depending on income. If you make "too much" money, your social security will be taxed. Too many retirees are shocked to find their social security benefits are subject to taxation. Fortunately, it's almost always possible to reduce social security taxes.

To reiterate, this is not an exhaustive list of retirement income tax schema. It's impossible to discuss every scenario here. But hopefully, it's clear that with a little forethought and planning, you can reduce your taxes. Taxes will always be there, but they shouldn't be a burden in retired life. Often, a proactive approach can greatly reduce your lifetime tax obligation.

The Tax Game Is a Long Game

If you're approaching retirement, or if you're already retired, you've probably been advised to capitalize on the benefits of tax-deferred accounts like 401(k)s, 403(b)s, 457s, IRAs, and TSPs. After all, that's where most people have stored their retirement savings. Tax planning is arguably *the* most important component of a retirement plan. You stand to sacrifice a lot of money if you don't prepare for taxes on your investment portfolio.

Many financial advisors preach deferment. "Defer, defer, defer," they say. "Delay taxes until you absolutely *must* pay them." Their logic appears sound. Presumably, the longer you can delay taxes, the lower they will eventually be. During your working years, your savings is free to compound without being reduced by taxes. And, if you happen to fall into a lower tax bracket after retirement, you will pay less in taxes than if you'd paid them when you still worked. At least, that's how it may have been in decades past.

Investors and soon-to-be retirees *must* realize that we are living in a unique economic climate, and it comes with a time stamp. Taxes are as low as they will probably ever be. On January 1, 2018, President Donald Trump's tax reform plan went into effect. It constituted the biggest change in tax law over the past three decades, and it has staggering implications for retirees and all investors alike. For one thing, the tax brackets and tax rates have been adjusted to the tax-payers' benefit. Also, the standard deduction for each tax bracket was sizably increased. If you don't think that taxes stand to increase by very much, consider the historical precedent. For the better part of the 20th century, the highest tax bracket was never lower than 70 percent. Following World War II and only ending in 1963, the highest tax bracket was a staggering 91 percent! Right now, it's only 37 percent. That leaves a lot of room for upward movement. https://taxfoundation.org/us-feder-al-individual-income-tax-rates-history-1913-2013-nominal-and-inflation-adjusted-brackets/

At some point, money in tax-deferred accounts will have to be paid. Taxes are likely to increase again in 2026. That means for many investors, it may be smart to pay taxes *now* while they're still inexpensive. There are, in fact, many reasons why deferment may not be the best course of action. But it's impossible to say what's best for you without a complete evaluation of your individual circumstances. One thing is certain though: taxes are lower now than they may ever be again. Act now to ensure you don't pay more in taxes than you owe. https://smartasset.com/taxes/heres-how-the-trump-tax-plan-could-affect-you

2018–2025 TAX BRACKETS

Single Filers	Married Filing Jointly	Tax Rate
$0–$9,525	$0–$19,050	10%
$9,526–$38,700	$19,051–$77,400	12%
$38,701–$82,500	$77,401–$165,000	22%
$82,501–$157,500	$165,001–$315,000	24%
$157,501–$200,000	$315,001–$400,000	32%

$200,001–$500,000	$400,001–$600,000	35%
$500,001+	$600,001+	37%

TAX YEAR 2017 STANDARD DEDUCTIONS

Single Filers	Married Filing Jointly
$6,350	$12,700

TAX YEAR 2018 (TRUMP PLAN) STANDARD DEDUCTIONS

Single Filers	Married Filing Jointly
$12,000	$24,000

Taxes on Social Security

As of this book's writing, retirees filing for taxes as single individuals are subject to taxation on 85 percent of their social security benefits if they earn more than $34,000. Couples are taxed the same if they earn at least $44,000. As you might imagine, that would come as a shock if a retiree expected his or her social security to go completely untaxed.

The key to reducing social security taxes is in understanding the IRS's definition of taxable income.

Then it's a game of mancala, moving your money around to avoid sitting in a higher tax bracket than necessary. In some cases, wise money management can even eliminate social security taxes. It all comes down to your provisional income.

Provisional income is what the IRS uses to determine taxation of social security. It consists of your total gross income (excluding social security), the tax-free interest you receive (this could be from municipal bonds, for example), and half of your social security benefits. If a married couple each receives $2,500 a month in social security benefits, right off the bat they start with $30,000 of provisional income annually. That's before additional income from part-time wages, pensions, capital gains, IRA distributions, or anything else.

Let's say, for the sake of illustration, that in retirement you earn $30,000 in returns on investments. That's your gross income. You also make $2,000 in interest on municipal bonds. Finally, you receive $24,000 from social security. Adding that all up (and remembering only to include *half* the social security benefit) gives you $44,000 in provisional income. A quick look at the table below shows that your social security is probably subject to taxation on up to 85 percent! What can you do to minimize those taxes?

Lower your income.

You probably just laughed for a minute before reading on. I understand; it sounds ridiculous. "Lower my income? What kind of advice is that!" But the trick is to lower *reportable* income without reducing any of the funds at your disposal. To do that, we need to adjust how your income is calculated.

Remember, provisional income (or taxable income) is the sum of your gross income, tax-free interest, and half of the social security benefits. *That's it.* Anything else falls outside the realm of IRS domain. So while stock market gains are lumped in with provisional income, income from things like annuity balances, which are tax-deferred, are not. Even if you reinvest stock market earnings, they must be reported as income, and you will be taxed on them. Instead, it may be prudent to move investment returns from a taxable category into one that is tax-favored. That could mean tax-deferred or something like a Roth IRA. The business of moving money around in this way can get messy if you don't know what you're doing, and you never want to compromise potential future earnings just to save a little in taxes now. It's best to consult with a qualified financial advisor before making such significant changes to your retirement portfolio.

Retirees often get confused by the variety of income sources. Social security, IRAs, 401(k)s, stock market gains—it can feel overwhelming. To maximize our resources and minimize our taxes, each part of our retirement portfolio should constitute a cog in the greater machine. When it comes to retirement income, it's best to think of it as just that—*one* income. Sure, it's funded by several investment assets, but everything ought to work together harmoniously to provide you with the most money possible. That's the bottom line.

Filing Status as of 2020	Provisional Income	SS Amount Subject to Tax
Married filing jointly	Under $32,000	0
	$32,000–$44,000	50%
	Over $44,000	85%
Single, head of household, qualifying widow(er), married filing separately & living apart from spouse	Under $25,000	0
	$25,000–$34,000	50%
	Over $34,000	85%
Married filing separately and living with spouse	Over 0	85%

One of the best ways to maximize your tax efficiency is to include Roth IRAs in your retirement strategy. Roth IRAs are such a powerful asset that really, they deserve a chapter of their own. But first, let's take a quick detour to examine the impact of required minimum distributions on your retirement prospects and some recent changes that may have eluded soon-to-be retirees.

CHAPTER 4

Required Minimum Distributions and the SECURE Act

If you've heard of required minimum distributions (RMDs), you probably remember them kicking in at age 70½ when the IRS forces you to begin taking distributions from your qualified retirement plans, such as IRAs, 401(k)s, 457 plans, 403(b) plans, and similar retirement plans.

Well, things have changed a bit recently. On January 1, 2020, President Donald Trump's SECURE Act went into effect. The legislation, which stands for Setting Every Community Up for Retirement Enhancement, was designed (as the laboriously contrived acronym suggests) to strengthen retirement security. It is supposed to achieve this through a number of new provisions and amendments to previous retirement standards. One of the biggest is the age at which RMDs start. The long-time age of 70½ has been changed to 72 in accordance with more current life expectancy data.

All tax-deferred accounts have one thing in common: You pay no taxes on the money you put into these plans, nor do you pay taxes on the interest you gain while they are growing. But when you begin withdrawing money from them, those withdrawals are considered ordinary income by the IRS and taxed accordingly. What if you never really need the money from any of these qualified plans? Can you just leave the money there and allow it to keep growing tax-deferred ad infinitum? No. That's where Uncle Sam's good ol' RMDs come into play. As soon as the ticker hits 72 years, you must withdraw a percentage of the balance of these accounts each year, and that percentage gets higher as you age.

The only exception to that rule is if you are still working for the company with which you have a 401(k). This presents an interesting opportunity.

Let's say you are working for a company—for the sake of example, we'll use General Motors—and you are 73 years old. Normally, you'd have been obligated to start RMDs a year earlier or face steep penalties of up to 50 percent of the money you should have withdrawn. But you're still working for GM. You have a 401(k) there, and let's also say you have other IRAs and retirement accounts. You would rather not have to take money out of those other accounts because you don't need the income right now. But because of your age, the IRS is forcing you to take money out of your other IRAs. You could actually take the money in your other qualified plans, roll it into your 401(k) at the company where you work, and not take any RMDs until you quit working. How's that for a trick?

Now, that isn't necessarily what you should do. You will need to discuss rolling money from one account to another with a qualified financial professional to make sure you are considering any potential fees, limits, or investment options specific to your situation. But there are many techniques like this with which you need to be familiar if you are interested in maximizing your retirement efficiency and minimizing your tax exposure; perfectly legal, perfectly ethical, and perfectly okay with the IRS.

The following table is what the IRS uses to determine your annual required distributions after age 72. You can see on the table that you simply take the total amount of all your IRAs (the December 31 value of the previous year) and divide by the distribution factor next to your age. That number is the amount of money you have to distribute from those retirement plans. You'll notice the chart still begins at age 70. That's because if you turned 70½ prior to January 1, 2020, your RMDs are still based on age 70½.

IRA Required MinimumDistribution

Age	Distribution Period	Age	Distribution Period
70	27.4	94	9.1
71	26.5	95	8.6
72	25.6	96	8.1
73	24.7	97	7.6
74	23.8	98	7.1
75	22.9	99	6.7
76	22.0	100	6.3
77	21.2	101	5.9
78	20.3	102	5.5
79	19.5	103	5.2
80	18.7	104	4.9
81	17.9	105	4.5
82	17.1	106	4.2
83	16.3	107	3.9
84	15.5	108	3.7
85	14.8	109	3.4
86	14.1	110	3.1
87	13.4	111	2.9
88	12.7	112	2.6
89	12.0	113	2.4
90	11.4	114	2.1
91	10.8	115+	1.9
92	10.2		
93	9.6		

The key here is to be proactive. Begin thinking about ways to gain control of your retirement accounts before you reach age 72. Let's say you are five years away from 72 and government-imposed RMDs. You should be coming up with a plan *now* to reduce the potential force out of those accounts once you reach the minimum age.

For instance, you may say, "Every time my IRA goes up in value, I'm going to start taking a little bit out so I don't create a bigger problem when I'm 72, potentially pushing me into a higher tax bracket or causing more of my Social Security income to become taxable."

What does that mean, specifically?

You may decide to convert money from your traditional tax-deferred retirement accounts to a Roth. This is kind of like "paying it forward." You may have to pay some additional taxes today, but then that Roth IRA is tax-free forever—even after you are gone. This strategy is especially advantageous if we believe tax rates will be higher in the future. But even if that turns out not to be the case and tax rates remain the same (not likely, see the previous chapter), think about your beneficiaries who may still be working and taking distributions from these accounts decades from today.

Keep in mind, I said "consider" converting some or all of your retirement accounts to Roth IRAs. I didn't say to go do it. You must sit down with a well-educated, well-rounded financial professional who is literate in these strategies and can walk you through the pros and cons of Roth conversion.

Remember, our objective is to protect ourselves against tax events. We may feel certain that taxes will be higher in the future than they are today, but neither you nor I have a crystal ball. We just don't know. But what we can do is control our taxable income every year. This may mean that we project what those required distributions will be when you are 72 and begin strategically converting tax-deferred dollars to Roth. That way, your taxable income won't go through the roof as you age. Instead, it will remain fairly steady.

Qualified Charitable Distributions

Due to major increases in the standard deduction under the Tax Cuts and Jobs Act—from $13,000 for a couple to $24,000 and $6,500 to $12,000 for single filers—many of those who may have historically itemized their deductions to capture mortgage interest deductions and charitable contributions (among other things) will no longer qualify for those deductions; they will not be larger than their standard deductions. This has presented a major planning opportunity for those interested in putting a few extra bucks back in their future pockets. Let me explain.

One of the more obvious options for those who are charitably inclined is to bunch their deductions in order to get over their standard deduction limits. In other words, you may want to set aside the amount you typically give into a separate account which you can give away as a lump sum in the future. For instance, if you typically tithe $5,000 per year, you may want to set aside $5,000 per year for five years and give $25,000 in a single year. This may also allow you to pick up other deductions you don't typically qualify for, such as mortgage interest and medical expenses.

On the other hand, maybe you don't have the discipline to set aside those funds without spending them for years in lieu of future deductions. In that case, if you are over 72, you're not out of luck yet. You may be able to take advantage of rules permitting a qualified charitable distribution, or QCD.

Rules allowing QCDs were originally created under Section 1201 of the Pension Protection Act of 2006; however, they were only effective for two years and lapsed. The rules were reinstated and lapsed several more times until 2015 legislation made the rules permanent. Now, as a result of the Tax Cuts and Jobs Act of 2017, these rules are becoming more popular than ever for retirees.

One benefit of doing a QCD from an IRA is the distribution comes out of the IRA without the tax consequences that would otherwise apply to the withdrawal. Most notably, there is no charitable deduction, but there is also no taxable income created in the first place, negating the need to itemize to qualify for the charitable deduction. By avoiding additional taxable income, you may also be able to avoid Social Security taxes or Medicare penalties you would have had if you hadn't contributed directly to the charity.

That said, the SECURE Act imposed some limitations on QCDs which could throw a wrench into your plans. The Act created a rule that limits the number of QCDs an IRA account holder can make. This was designed to prevent abuse of the provision. But it has unfortunately made the strategy more complicated to use even for savvy investors with honorable intentions. The best way to ensure that your strategy will work to your tax and retirement advantage is to enlist the skill and experience of a financial professional. https://www.kiplinger.com/article/retirement/T054-C000-S004-secure-act-changes-squeeze-qcds.html

At this point, you may still have some lingering questions about IRAs and tax efficiency. That's understandable. The next chapter will summarize what we've learned so far, expound on the benefits of IRAs, and answer some frequently asked questions.

CHAPTER 5

IRAs and Frequently Asked Questions

So far in this book, I've often discussed IRAs with respect to other retirement planning principles. But it's about time we give the IRA some attention of its own.

I'm sure you've heard of IRAs, but you may not be familiar with their many variations. Over time, the IRA has evolved into a category of retirement investments more than a singular investment vehicle. One of the most significant IRA types is the **Roth IRA**.

Some politicians have bridges and streets named after them, which serve to memorialize them for years after they die. The late US senator William V. Roth has something much better—the Roth IRA.

The senator was a fiscal conservative who viewed taxes, for the most part, as the anathema of economic growth. A strong advocate of tax cuts, he co-authored the Economic Recovery Tax Act of 1981. His idea was that the less we have to pay in taxes, the more we will spend and save; that, in turn, will stimulate the economy, generating more revenue for the government in the long run than a direct tax would have.

It is no wonder, then, that while he saw the IRA as a good way to help individuals save for retirement, he also wanted to tweak it to eliminate the tax on the back end. Essentially, his philosophy was "Let's go ahead and pay the taxes on the contribution side and be done with it. But let it grow tax-free, and let us withdraw it tax-free." So the Taxpayer Relief Act of 1997 expanded on the traditional IRA to offer that flexibility, and the Roth IRA was born.

Today, Roth IRAs can be set up at banks, brokerage firms, and insurance companies. They allow for early withdrawal of your original contribution without penalties and withdrawal of the earnings tax-free after a five-year waiting period and after the owner turns 59½ years old. The earnings generated from the original Roth IRA contribution can also be withdrawn early, but they are subject to penalties.

The money invested in a Roth IRA has already been taxed, so any return you earn on your Roth IRA investments won't be taxed, as long as you wait until at least age 59½ to withdraw your profits. By contrast, traditional IRA contributions and earnings are taxed as income upon withdrawal. Just remember, a traditional IRA contribution is tax-deductible; a Roth IRA contribution isn't.

The beauty of the IRA, in general, is that you're free to invest the money in your IRA however you choose. Some common Roth IRA investment options are common stocks, index funds, bonds, certificates of deposit (CDs), and real estate investment trusts (REITs). The flexibility that comes with being able to invest in your Roth IRA as you choose, as well as to withdraw funds early or leave them invested long after your 71st birthday, has contributed to its growing popularity.

Does age play a role in Roth IRA contributions? You bet it does! As of 2013, a 25-year-old can contribute a maximum of $5,500 annually to a Roth IRA (the limit was $5,000 in 2012). If you are over 50, you can do another $1,000. Even though older people can contribute more, younger people have an advantage when investing in a Roth IRA because their contributions have the potential to grow significantly over the years. Let's say a 25-year-old deposited $5,000 in a Roth IRA and that's all he or she ever invested, and let's say the account earned 8 percent annually. He or she would have $7,346.63 after 5 years—tax-free! In 10 years, the amount would more than double to $10,794.61— tax-free! It seems like a no-brainer, doesn't it? Imagine how much that initial $5,000 investment would make over the 34 years it would take to reach maturity. Oh, the power of compounded interest!

Now, I'm not going to say that senior Americans wouldn't benefit from contributing to a Roth IRA. It's just that because of the time value of money and the effects of compound interest, younger people have an edge.

Let's say someone over 50 makes a one-time contribution of $6,000 to a Roth IRA and earns 8 percent interest annually. He or she would have $12,953.52 tax-free income available after 10 years. No, that's probably not enough to retire on, but keep in mind there is no law against contributing the maximum amount allowed by law to the account every year and letting that compound as well.

Oh yes, another benefit of contributing to a Roth IRA is that there's no mandatory withdrawal date. As all owners of traditional IRAs who have reached the age of 70½ know, they must begin making withdrawals—even if they don't need the money. These withdrawals are called required minimum distributions, or RMDs. You can wait as long as you like to withdraw money from your Roth IRA, if you even want to at all. Can your beneficiaries inherit a Roth IRA with no penalties attached? Yes.

As the need for retirement savings increased, additional plans were created, like the 401(a), 401(k), 457, SEP IRA, and others. These plans allow individuals to grow their retirement savings on a tax-deferred basis. All of these plans result in taxable consequences for beneficiaries, with the exception of the Roth IRA, which is income tax free to both owners and heirs upon withdrawal.

Keep in mind retirement is the end game, which, as every chess player knows, is the time when you must remain alert and focused. During the accumulation phase of your life, you worked hard to put money into these accounts and saw it grow. Hopefully, you reached your savings goal. Now during the distribution years, your goal is—or should be—to keep what you have earned or at least to keep as much of it as you can. What good is it, after all, to make it to the summit if you lose everything on your way down?

Since IRA rules are constantly changing, you need to either be diligent in studying them or find a financial advisor who specializes in IRAs. An IRA specialist will be up to date on the rules and able to advise you. Make sure when you interview an advisor you find out if they specialize in IRA planning.

Frequently Asked IRA Questions

If you are in or approaching the distribution phase, here are some questions you may have about IRAs:

1. Should I roll over my 401(k), 403(b), or other employer-provided retirement plan to an IRA?

2. Should I wait until age 72 to take distributions?

3. What if I want to leave my IRA to my children? What is the best way to do that?

4. Doesn't my will or trust dictate where my IRA funds go after my death?

5. How is the settlement of an IRA inheritance handled?

6. Wait, what happened to stretch IRAs?

FAQ #1: Should I roll over my 401(k), 403(b), or other employer-provided retirement plan to an IRA?

Let's say you have a 401(k), 403(b), or other company-sponsored retirement plan, but you no longer work for the employer or you are going to leave that place of employment. What are your options?

First of all, you *could* take the money in cash, but *please* don't do that. Big mistake! There's no debating that. But chances are if you are reading this book, you are intelligent enough to know that. Taxes are due on the entire amount when you file your return for the year you took the withdrawal. That could be 35 percent of the total at the federal level, plus more in state tax. If you aren't yet 59½, there's an additional 10 percent penalty tax on the full amount. Uncle Sam will love you, but you will hate yourself in the morning.

Secondly, you could just leave the account right where it is. Some people do that because it is the easiest thing to do. No decisions to make. I get that, but do you really want those folks in your old personnel office, or their selected custodians, making the decisions about your money? Did you know that some plans charge higher fees on inactive accounts (i.e., once you stop making contributions)? Also, some plans will not allow you to change your allocations if your account is inactive; you'd have to stick with the investments you selected before you left your previous employer. I know of some individuals who thought that keeping their money in the company plan provided them with some sort of a group discount. But that is rarely the case, even with very large corporations.

So I suppose the short answer to the question "Should I roll my 401(k) account over to an IRA?" is yes. That way you will be in control of where and how your money is invested. Of course, it may not matter; if the balance is less than $5,000, your former employer may require you to move it.

There are several other reasons why rolling a 401(k) over to an IRA is a good idea:

- **401(k) investment options are often limited.** Most 401(k) plans offer few investment options—usually 9 or 10 mutual funds, whereas an IRA can open up thousands of investment options. You can choose IRAs that will allow much more frequent trading than a company plan allows. In an IRA, you can invest in mutual funds, individual stocks, exchange-traded funds, annuities, CDs, money market funds, and the list goes on.

- **IRA distributions can be deferred for up to 10 years for non-spouse beneficiaries, whereas a 401(k) plan cannot.** If a beneficiary inherits a 401(k) account and does not roll it over into an inherited IRA, he or she will most likely have to pay all the taxes as a lump sum. However, with an inherited IRA rollover, the beneficiary can continue to defer taxes for up to 10 years. With a company-sponsored plan, the company sets the rules governing the plan. Even if the plan currently allows certain benefits for the next generation, the company can change that rule at any time.

- **Most 401(k) plans do not allow conversion to a Roth IRA.** With a Roth IRA, money grows tax-free and can be withdrawn tax-free. This can be a huge advantage if future tax rates go up. The tax laws may eventually allow for Roth IRA conversions directly from 401(k) plans, but in the meantime, converting to a traditional IRA enables you to control the account, including your potential decision to convert it to a Roth IRA.

- **401(k) plan fees are hard to understand.** With a 401(k), the plan document is the rule book. The company chooses the investment options and sets the fees. As I write this, the government is working to make these fees more transparent, but do you want to allow your previous employer to control the fees you pay? Probably not. With a rollover IRA, you choose the investment options and the fees you pay. In other words, you get to write the rule book.

These are just a few of the reasons to roll over your employer-sponsored 401(k) into an IRA. In fact, I can think of only one reason not to do so, and it applies to people between the ages of 55 and 59. At age 55, most 401(k) plans allow an individual to withdraw funds without a 10 percent tax penalty. With IRAs, you have to be 59½ to withdraw funds without a tax penalty. So if you are in that age group and know you will need income from the account, it may be wise to leave your funds in the company plan. You may find it advantageous to borrow money from the account and pay it back rather than outright withdraw it, too. Paying needless penalties is like setting fire to cash. What a waste!

How to do a 401(k) rollover

Rolling over a 401(k) can seem intimidating. There are a few things to consider. First, you need to select a custodian for your IRA. You will have to park the money with a financial institution of some description. Some popular choices are Schwab, Fidelity, Scottrade, and TD Ameritrade; it could even be your local bank or credit union.

If you don't already have an IRA, the next step is usually to open an account with your new custodian. You will want to ask them for the exact payee name your 401(k) provider should put on the distribution check, as well as the address they (or you) should mail it to.

Once you have this information, contact your current 401(k) provider. You may be able to initiate the transfer right over the phone. Other providers will require that you fill out a rollover form.

I always recommend that my clients do a trustee-to-trustee transfer. You will have to indicate the destination to which the employer-sponsored account is to be transferred, whether it is to your new account or an existing IRA. A trustee-to-trustee transfer, if done properly, eliminates the possibility of triggering a tax.

How to do a trustee-to-trustee transfer

A trustee-to-trustee transfer means that the check for the funds in your employer-sponsored account is made out to the new institution with which you are setting up your IRA. When you do a trustee-to-trustee transfer, there is no limit to the number of transfers you can do. If you do what is called a *60-day rollover*, you are limited to only one rollover per year.

The 60-day rollover rule

This rule applies when the check for the funds in the employee-sponsored account is made out to you. You must deposit the funds into an IRA within 60 days or you will trigger some events that I am quite sure you will find financially unpleasant. The IRS will view the amount as ordinary income and treat it as such. You will be required to include the entire amount transferred as income on your tax return, and you will be taxed at your current, ordinary income tax rate. Plus, if you are not over the age of 59½, you will pay a 10 percent penalty on the withdrawal. Are there any exceptions? Yes, a few:

- Taxable distributions of up to $10,000 from your IRAs are not subject to the 10 percent early distribution penalty if the IRA owner or a qualified family member is a first-time homebuyer and, within 120 days of receipt, the amount is used for qualifying acquisition or rebuilding costs for a principal residence. If the amount withdrawn is not used because of a cancellation or delay in the purchase or construction of the residence, you have 120 days to roll it back into the IRA instead of the usual 60 days.

- If you make a deposit error during the roll-over process, you may be exempt from the penalty. I suppose the government realizes that mistakes can be made. But you have to be able to prove that the money was delivered to the financial institution within the 60-day window and prove that a legitimate error was made. "I forgot" and "I had a flat tire" are not legitimate excuses.

Perhaps you can see why I recommend the trustee-to-trustee transfer instead of having the check cut to you, even though you do have 60 days to redeposit it. If this entire process seems a bit complicated, don't despair. It will be worth it once you complete the task and have your own plan under your control. Fortunately, most financial institutions and financial planners can guide you through the process one step at a time if you need help.

FAQ #2: Should I wait until age 72 to take distributions?

There is no cut-and-dried answer to this question. It may depend on a number of factors and individual circumstances, but here are some things to consider.

Assume you are 60 years old and have $500,000 in your IRA. If you earn a modest 6 percent rate of return, your account value will be $1,006,098 at age 72.

To calculate your RMD, you would divide $1,006,098 by the remaining number of years you have to live according to the IRS, which, at age 72, is 25.6 years (see Table in Chapter 4). This means your required yearly distribution will be $39,300.71 ($1,006,098 ÷ 25.6). This amount will add to your adjusted gross income and could put you into a higher tax bracket.

Extending your distributions over a longer time frame would help you avoid such a big jump in income. For example, assume you start taking $20,000 per year from the IRA at age 60 and convert those funds to a Roth IRA. The Roth IRA would allow your money to grow tax-free *with no RMDs*! With this approach, at age 72, your traditional IRA would have approximately $668,000 in it, and your RMD would be $26,093. This difference could potentially keep you in a lower tax bracket. In addition, you would also have a Roth IRA with a balance of $357,000, equaling a grand total between the two accounts of $1,025,000! True, this would require you to pay some tax along the way. But it is important to understand that someone will eventually pay those taxes. This strategy is not advisable if you feel your future taxes will be lower. However, it is a strategy to consider if, like me and most other Americans, you believe your future taxes will almost certainly be higher.

FAQ #3: What if I want to leave my IRA to my children? What is the best way to do that?

When an IRA passes to the next generation, it is the beneficiary—not the original owner or the estate—who is responsible for the taxes due on the inheritance. IRAs and retirement accounts have a different set of tax rules than real estate, savings accounts, or even stocks.

IRA inheritance income taxes usually come as a shocking surprise. Unfortunately, most families never sit down and discuss these things. In fact, many IRA owners are not even aware they are leaving something behind that can cause so much trouble. Would it surprise you to learn that the IRA you leave behind for your loved ones could be reduced by 40 percent or more due to taxes? This could be prevented with a little more education about inherited IRAs.

The fact of the matter is when an IRA inheritance is withdrawn immediately, the taxes can create immediate and enormous losses of wealth. Let's say you leave a $300,000 IRA to your son, Bob, who earns $50,000 per year. As soon as Bob deposits the check, his income immediately jumps up to $350,000. What does that do to his tax bracket? It puts him in the highest bracket possible. That's why Uncle Sam often becomes the most highly rewarded beneficiary of inherited IRAs. I don't have to tell you this, but losing nearly half of your inheritance and later finding out that you could have avoided it is not pleasant!

What is a stretch IRA? Well, it's nothing anymore. The stretch IRA used to be a nice solution to the aforementioned problem, but it no longer exists. You can still benefit from some of its features though. See the final FAQ in this chapter.

The tax-free benefits of an inherited Roth IRA

When viewed as a multi-generational financial investment, the Roth IRA can be extremely valuable. Few people grasp the wealth-building potential of these accounts for heirs who inherit them as inherited Roth IRAs. It adds up to a great deal more than simply leaving a tax-free inheritance. When passed to the next generation, a inherited Roth IRA can continue to compound tax free, just as it did during the life of the original owner.

Like a regular inherited IRA, an RMD must be taken from the account using the IRS table for IRA beneficiaries (see Table I in Appendix A). The major difference is that distributions from an inherited Roth IRA are income tax free to the beneficiaries! Even if taken as a lump-sum distribution, withdrawals are tax-free. Because they don't see the power of tax-free growth in a compounding account, most beneficiaries do not keep the funds in an inherited Roth IRA. They take the money and fun—I mean run!

Consider this: All earnings inside and distributed from an inherited Roth IRA are tax-free to the beneficiary. Suppose you are the beneficiary and you are quite good at investing. You inherit a $10,000 Roth IRA and through wise investments, you increase the account balance to $500,000. The entire $500,000 is tax-free upon withdrawal! Did the word *WOW!* and a yellow light bulb just appear in the cartoon thought bubble over your head like it did in mine when I first realized this? I hope so, because that clearly demonstrates the true value and financial power of a inherited Roth IRA.

FAQ #4: Doesn't my will or trust dictate where my IRA funds go after my death?

The short answer is no. The distribution of IRA funds is governed by the IRA beneficiary form, regardless of who your will or trust names as your heirs. The *designated beneficiary* line on an IRA form is the same as the *beneficiary line* on an insurance policy form. Because it is a contract, the IRA beneficiary form trumps wills and trusts when it comes to estate settlement. That's why it's so important to update these documents when life circumstances change.

Properly naming beneficiaries

Your IRA assets can be considerably diminished by probate costs and excessive taxes if you do not have properly named beneficiaries. You must name two categories of beneficiaries: primary and contingent. Upon the owner's death, the account is divided among the primary beneficiaries. The division may be by a dollar amount or by percentage. If the type of division has not been indicated on the beneficiary form, the financial institution typically divides the account evenly among all living primary beneficiaries.

If there are no living primary beneficiaries, the funds are paid to contingent beneficiaries. If no contingent beneficiary has been named, the account goes to the estate and enters probate, which can be a time-consuming, costly, and unpleasant process. **Be certain you have named a contingent beneficiary on your tax-deferred retirement accounts.** Typically, couples with children will name the spouse as the primary beneficiary and the children as contingent beneficiaries.

Per stirpes and per capita

Can you accidentally disinherit a loved one? Absolutely! How? By simply not specifying in your documents how you want your wealth parceled out. By not using either *per capita* or *per stirpes* designations, it is possible that your IRA may not go to your intended beneficiaries.

Per stirpes is not an expression we use in everyday speech, but it is a valuable phrase to understand when it comes to how you plan to distribute the wealth you leave behind. It is a legal term that in Latin literally means "per branch" or "by the roots." Per stirpes specifies that each branch of the deceased person's family receives an equal share of the estate, regardless of how many people are in that branch. For example, if A and B are the children of the deceased but B is also deceased, leaving children C, D, E, F, and G (the grandchildren of the original person), then A would receive one half of the estate, and each of B's five children would receive one-tenth of the estate (essentially, they are dividing B's half).

Let's say you have two children, Tim and Catherine. Tim has four children and Catherine has none. While Tim and Catherine are alive, your IRA would be split evenly between them when you die. However, your intention is for Tim's share of the inherited IRA to go to his children if Tim dies before you do. If Tim dies first and then you die, without any special notation on the IRA beneficiary form, your grandchildren would be disinherited and the entire IRA would go to Catherine. To prevent this from happening, use the words *per stirpes* after Tim's name on the beneficiary designation form. Without this notation, the IRA will pass per capita and will be shared among the other living beneficiaries.

Per capita is a legal term that means "by the head" in Latin. In the context of inheritance distribution, it weights each person rather than each branch of the family. As the example above demonstrates, it is easy to disinherit a beneficiary unwittingly. Most financial institutions assume a per capita distribution, meaning they will pay out the IRA only to living beneficiaries upon the owner's death. If Tim and Catherine had no children, the issue of per capita or per stirpes would be of no concern.

The key takeaway of this is that most financial institutions assume per capita designations unless otherwise indicated in the language of the document in question. Speak with a legal professional if you need more information. Since one wrong decision can lead to expensive consequences, it is a good idea to talk to a financial advisor who has an attorney on staff before either making a move that you will later regret or omitting an action that you should have taken.

Living trusts and IRAs

Most families assume a living trust will manage the entire estate burden upon the death of a loved one. For IRAs, this is not true. A living trust has many purposes. For example, a correctly drafted living trust can protect your estate from federal estate taxes. These are the taxes assessed by the government on the entire estate. You may need to consult an estate advisor to determine whether estate taxes will be a concern for you. Beyond estate taxes, income taxes on IRAs are due from the beneficiary, regardless of the estate size.

The primary function of trusts is to protect from probate any assets that do not automatically bypass that process. A trust may help avoid probate on assets like homes, brokerage accounts, investment properties, and bank accounts. But with IRAs, the way to avoid probate is to make sure you have properly named your beneficiary(ies).

You may have a good reason to name a trust as the beneficiary. One reason might be a special needs child who will require a trustee to administer funds. Another reason you may want your trustee to control the distributions is that you do not wish to hand over full control to your heirs. Yet another reason may be that you have a very large estate. Whatever your reason, you must have your trust specially drafted to take full advantage of this option.

Leaving an IRA to charity

If you are charitably inclined, you may wish to leave your tax-deferred wealth to charity. Assets like real estate receive a step-up in tax basis at death. Because of this, there are no taxes due upon the sale or liquidation of assets at your death. On the other hand, beneficiaries of tax-deferred IRAs owe taxes on the account upon the owner's death.

If you plan to donate a portion of your estate to charity, consider leaving an IRA. Charities typically do not pay taxes, so they would not owe taxes upon the inheritance of these accounts. You can also avoid giving an asset with a tax liability to your family by bequeathing your tax-deferred IRA to charity.

Keep your beneficiary forms updated

Death, birth, divorce, remarriage—these are common changes that occur in a family. If one of these changes takes place, review your beneficiary elections on your retirement accounts. Many times children or grandchildren are born after beneficiary forms are filled out. If this happens, update your beneficiary designations so that no one is accidentally excluded.

I often recommend that clients who own IRAs have a family meeting to let their beneficiaries know what to expect when they inherit this type of asset. It is actually a sensitive, loving, and courteous thing to do. If you were kind enough to include them as the inheritors of your assets, why not be kind enough to help them avoid the confusion that can accompany inheriting an IRA?

A discussion with your heirs now will prepare them for what to expect later. It can even be used as a prelude to a social gathering. No law against that! The modern age we live in can bring us face-to-face with our relatives in a click of a button, too, through video conferencing on our computers, tablets, and smartphones. Or just schedule an old-fashioned conference call. Your financial advisor should be able to provide you with the bullet points you need to discuss. Some may even provide you with a nicely bound notebook for each of your beneficiaries to let them know what to expect.

FAQ #5: How is the settlement of an IRA inheritance handled?

To begin settling IRAs upon the death of the owner, the estate executor, trustee, or beneficiary should contact the financial institution that holds the account. Financial institutions have different procedures for settling IRAs. Most will require a verifiable death certificate. Once they verify the death of the IRA owner, they will contact and freely correspond with the named beneficiaries.

Note: *If there are multiple beneficiaries, it is essential that the IRA be segregated into separate accounts before any distributions are made. Failure to do so can result in a loss of the inheritied IRA option and subsequent income tax benefits. After accounts are segregated, beneficiaries can decide how to settle their individual shares.*

IRAs can avoid probate if beneficiaries have been properly designated. The IRA funds will pass directly to named beneficiaries without being exposed to public scrutiny and the customary foot-dragging of the courts in settling estates.

Year of death RMD

What happens when an IRA owner dies after turning 72 but before taking the RMD? A distribution must be taken from the account and paid to the beneficiary, who is then responsible for the taxes on the distribution. The financial institution will tell you if this is a matter of concern. Of course, if the IRA was a Roth IRA, no minimum distributions are required for the deceased owner; however, a non-spouse beneficiary must withdraw all the funds from the Roth IRA by the 10th year.

Beneficiary determination date

By September 30 of the year following the year of death of the IRA owner, all beneficiaries must be finalized. The purpose of this deadline—also known as the *designation date*—is to give beneficiaries time to decide if they want to disclaim or decline their share of the IRA inheritance.

Proper segregation of the IRA

The IRA must be segregated into separate accounts representing each beneficiary's share by December 31 of the year after the year of the IRA owner's death. This enables each beneficiary to either defer payments up to 10 years or begin payments at their desired amount.

Qualified disclaimers

If a beneficiary wants to disclaim an IRA inheritance, it must be done in writing and generally by the designation date. Some beneficiaries choose to disclaim an inheritance to better manage wealth within the family. This strategy allows a beneficiary to pass on some or all of an inherited IRA to the next named beneficiary.

As an example, a father could name his daughter as a primary beneficiary and her children (his grandchildren) as contingent beneficiaries. If the daughter happens to be well-off financially and has no need for the IRA inheritance, she could disclaim it. The IRA would then pass on to her children, the contingent beneficiaries.

Assuming the daughter had a large estate or no need for the funds from the inheritance, the disclaimer would allow her to avoid increasing her estate and potentially increasing her tax burden. Naturally, the daughter's children would have a longer life expectancy, so the value of the inherited IRA calculated over their lives could be considerably greater in terms of the total lifetime income distributions.

The decision to disclaim should not be made lightly. A disclaimer is an irrevocable decision to give up your right to inherit IRA assets. You cannot change your mind once that decision has been executed.

Note: *The primary beneficiary does not get to choose the person they wish to disclaim to. Whoever ultimately receives the IRA inheritance is dictated by the beneficiary election form completed by the owner. If the primary beneficiary disclaims the inheritance, it will go to the next listed contingent beneficiary.*

Settlement options when the spouse is the primary beneficiary of an IRA are clearly spelled out by the IRS code:

1. **Spousal continuation.** When it comes to inheriting an IRA, spouses can basically treat the account as their own. Let's say a wife inherits her husband's IRA. If she wishes, she can let the money continue to grow in the IRA. If it's a traditional IRA, she will be forced to take RMDs when she reaches age 72. If the spouse inherits a Roth IRA, no distributions will be required, ever. The only little wrinkle is that if she were to elect to treat the account as her own, any distributions taken before age 59½ could be subject to the 10 percent early withdrawal penalty. Spouses are able to roll inherited IRAs into accounts of their own that are retitled in their name. This resets everything. Now they can name their own beneficiaries and make any other associated determinations. If the deceased spouse was over the age of 72 and taking RMDs at the time of his or her death, then the RMD for the year of death must be made before rolling the account into the name of the surviving spouse. After the rollover, the surviving spouse will use his or her own

age to determine the amount of all future RMDs. Again, no RMDs are required for Roth IRAs, ever.

2. **Inherited IRA.** Spouses may receive the account as an inherited IRA and take distributions immediately or defer payments for up to 10 years. Surviving spouses who elect this option do not have to take a distribution unless the IRA owner would have turned 72.

3. **Disclaimers.** A spouse named as the primary beneficiary has the right to disclaim some or all of the IRA assets and pass them on to the next generation. Before choosing this option, be sure to review who the deceased spouse listed as beneficiaries and complete a new beneficiary election form.

4. **Full liquidation.** A spouse can close (liquidate) the account and pay taxes on the income. There will be no taxes due if the account is a Roth IRA. Unless funds are needed, however, this may not be the wisest option. Closing the account means losing the numerous aforementioned benefits that a inherited IRA can provide.

The IRS also clearly outlines three basic IRA settlement options for non-spouse beneficiaries (children, siblings, parents, and friends):

1. **Full liquidation.** Although few who are knowledgeable about the tax consequences of this option would recommend it, beneficiaries can choose to cash out their IRA inheritance. As previously mentioned, this distribution is considered income, which will be added to the rest of the beneficiary's household income unless it is from a Roth IRA. Taxes will be due and payable. Electing the lump-sum cash-out can push the beneficiary into a higher tax bracket and result in a higher tax bill. Again, this option also eliminates all the benefits of a inherited IRA.

2. **Inherited IRA.** The second option is to leave the IRA in its tax-deferred state. Beneficiaries will not be required to take an annual RMD. This option allows beneficiaries to minimize income taxes and grow their inheritances into significantly larger sums of money. However, the IRA funds are required to be 100% liquidated by the tenth year following the death of the original IRA owner. As previously discussed, an inherited IRA provides beneficiaries with the most

withdrawal flexibility. Even more importantly, beneficiaries could end up with significantly more money due to the continued tax-deferred growth of the account. This can be a significant benefit, especially for tax-free Roth IRAs.

3. **Disclaimers.** This option allows the primary beneficiary to pass on some or all of the IRA to the named contingent beneficiaries, who can then inherit it as an inherited IRA.

FAQ #6: Wait, what happened to the Stretch IRA?

Ah, the stretch IRA. Everyone has heard of it, but few understood how it worked. It's a moot point now, though. As one MarketWatch article put it, "The SECURE act killed the Stretch IRA."

The Stretch IRA was a wonderful provision whereby non-spousal inheritors of an IRA could withdraw its assets tax-free over the course of their lifetime. Sadly, this provision no longer exists.

Nowadays, beneficiaries must withdraw the total sum of funds within an IRA within 10 years of inheriting it. If they fail to do this, they must pay taxes on everything all at once. In case it's not obvious, *do not* fail to withdraw every cent from your inherited IRA inside of the 10-year block. The tax ramifications for waiting too long aren't worth the trouble.

Get Professional Assistance!

As you can see, IRAs can be powerful financial-planning tools capable of accumulating large sums of tax-deferred funds to pay for retirement or other family needs. When properly constructed using the right investment mix and custodian, an IRA can be the perfect receptacle for much of your net worth. Few other financial tools afford the investor the flexibility, control, and portability of an IRA. But like many useful financial tools, they come with their own brand of complexity.

I once was invited by a pilot friend of mine to sit behind the controls of a Cessna Citation jet aircraft often used for personal travel by corporate executives. I gazed in wonder at all of the dials, switches, and gauges.

"Do you know what every one of these controls does?" I asked.

"Of course," he replied. "If I didn't, I couldn't fly the plane."

That made perfect sense, of course. Then he explained to me that it was like learning anything else. He recounted how he had spent many hours in the classroom and in the cockpit with a qualified instructor before he felt at ease flying the swift and complex jet.

The complexity of IRAs may seem to the uninitiated observer as baffling as the controls in the cockpit of that jet. Just as we leave the flying to professionals when we travel by air, so should we lean on the expertise of financial professionals when making decisions regarding IRAs—especially if we want to maximize their use for our legacy and retirement planning.

Even financial professionals, however, must specialize in this area of planning to be effective; the rules are always changing. How much do you need to know about how your IRA works? That's up to you. But I encourage IRA owners to get as much education about their accounts as possible—at least to the point where they feel confident that their IRAs are invested wisely and structured to their best advantage. This may require a little effort, but the payoff could be well worth it for both you and your heirs.

CHAPTER 6

What Drives the US Economy?

O ne of the biggest questions on the minds of retirees these days is "Where is the economy headed?"
If you are a retiree or are approaching retirement, then
I don't blame you for asking the question. After all,
the direction in which the economy moves at the juncture of your retirement could very well determine how
prosperous you will be in your golden years. Granted,
when it comes to a successful retirement, money isn't
everything, but it may be what we worry about the
most. If you don't think economic concerns are wide-
spread these days, just go to your Google search bar
and type in the phrase "where is the economy headed";
you will see more than 20 million results come up.

I was at an airport recently and wanted to pick
up something to read before my flight, so I strolled

over to the newsstand nearest to my gate assignment. First of all, I was amazed at just the number of magazines that are in print. The rack took up an entire wall that was at least 20 feet wide, with hundreds of magazines collectively covering every subject under the sun. Among them were at least 20 magazines having to do with finance and investment. I recognized some: *Kiplinger's, Money, Fortune, Smart Money*. But there were some I had never heard of. As if they were all competing for my attention, the headlines screamed urgencies like:

"Get Ready for the Next Big Crash"

"Buy Gold Now"

"15 Stocks to Buy NOW!"

"What to Do with Your Mutual Funds NOW"

"Why the Market Will Soar"

"Invest in the New Tech Revolution"

I came away with the clear impression that you could find just about any investing philosophy you wanted to find on this rack of magazines, and none of them, despite their claims otherwise, knew what was going to happen in the future. These authors and publishers just wanted to sell magazines. The plain truth is there is no silver bullet. What will happen with the economy is anyone's guess, and no one has a crystal ball (not one that works, anyway). I would pay good money to see this idea put forth on a magazine cover:

"We Do Not Know What's Going to Happen with the Economy"

That wouldn't sell too many magazines, would it? How about economists? Do they know where the economy is heading? The short answer is no. If you read articles written by economists, you may come away feeling more confused. While one economist predicts that we're ready for a big expansion, another declares that a great retraction is just around the corner. Without getting caught up in an exhausting string of numbers and conflicting opinions, let me share with you a big-picture view that is not designed to tell you how the market will move in the next month, or even the next six months, but instead may provide a useful overview of how things could look in the coming years.

What Makes Up the US Economy?

To start with the basics, the measure used to determine the state of the US economy is the gross domestic product or GDP. What makes up the GDP?

GDP = personal consumption

+ gross investment

+ government spending

+ (exports − imports)

Personal consumption makes up 70 percent of the GDP, so let's focus on that. Plainly stated, personal consumption is what people spend their money on—things like food, clothing, housing, recreation, services, appliances, transportation, and health care.

If you look at a graph of personal consumption data from 1982 to 2008, you will see that it increased year after year. Then an interesting thing happened in 2009: personal spending declined. If you are mentally connecting the dots, you are thinking, "Well, sure. There was a stock market crash, and a big recession began that year. It seems logical that there would be a drop in personal spending." But that's not the whole picture. Think back to 2001 and 2002. The US stock market had a major decline in those years too. The nation was attacked by terrorists on September 11, 2001, and a war on terrorism started with military action in Afghanistan and Iraq. Yet there was no decline in personal consumption.

If personal consumption is responsible for more than 70 percent of the US economy, then it is important to analyze this phenomenon. Since fluctuations in personal consumption can make the US economy either expand or contract, we need to try to figure out if there is a pattern here that could give us a clue as to what is likely to happen in the future.

Statistically, people spend the most between the ages of 45 and 54. Why? Because they have families. It's between the ages of 45 and 54 that child-related expenses are highest. Parents are paying for their kids' college educations, as well as buying them cars and other large-ticket items.

Next, take a look at the demographics involved. Baby boomers make up one of the largest segments of the US population. The United States Census Bureau considers a baby boomer to be someone born between 1946 and 1964. There are an estimated 73 million US baby boomers at the time of this writing. Unless you arrived on the last load of coconuts, you know what a huge impact this massive horde of home and car buyers, theatergoers, restaurant patrons, clothes shoppers (and on and on) have made and are making on the personal consumption element of the GDP!

Remember the big economic boom that started in the 1990s? The oldest of the baby boom generation were turning 45 at the rate of 10,000 per day back in 1991. They were entering the biggest spending phase of their lives, and as a result, the US economy became an unstoppable juggernaut. Not even a terrorist attack, a recession, and the bursting of the tech bubble could stop it. After all, these hard-working baby boomers had to put kids through college and buy bigger homes, newer cars, and large-ticket items...until they began entering the next phase of their lives—retirement.

The oldest of the baby boom generation turned 65 in 2011. That means the majority of them have already lived through their biggest spending years. An estimated 34 million baby boomers are now living in retirement. Think about yourself, your neighbors, and your friends. What is the next financial goal after the kids are out of school and you are 55 or older?

Retirement! Around age 55, you begin the savings phase of life, preparing for retirement. Is there any kind of government stimulus that will motivate you to increase your spending? No! You're like squirrels when they know that winter is coming. You are saving everything. You want to retire, and you have only a few years to get ready.

This phase-of-life change for the baby boom generation is one of the main reasons for the decline in consumer spending that began in 2009, and this trend will continue as the remaining baby boomers enter the savings phase of their lives up until 2031. Thus, it only makes sense that the economy will slow as consumer demand continues to decline. This, in turn, will affect stock prices. And as manufacturers and those in the services industry adjust to this restricted spending, we will likely see higher unemployment than usual.

But there is a bright side to this story. Baby boomers had babies. Another large generation is coming along—not as large as the baby boom generation, but another generation nonetheless—with kids of their own and money in their pockets. We refer to them as Generation Y or "echo boomers." The echo boomers are unlikely to have the spending impact the baby boomers had, but they are around 60 million strong and will eventually create economic growth again. It will take a few years before that cycle happens.

It is interesting to note that this same type of cycle occurred in the Japanese economy in the early

'90s. Japan's equivalent of the US baby boom generation is older. Japan's baby boomers moved into their spending phase in the '70s, and their economy boomed in the '70s and '80s. The Japanese Nikkei 225 (similar to the US Dow Jones Industrial Average) skyrocketed from 10,000 in 1984 to nearly 40,000 in early 1990. Then their baby boom generation began to enter their savings phase of life. What do you think happened? Their economy started to slow down. Consider that in 1995 the Nikkei 225 was at 20,000. By 2001, it had fallen to 10,000. That's a 75 percent drop in value from the peak over roughly a decade. In the same period, home values fell drastically.

Everyone knows that when the economy starts to slow down, all you need is a government stimulus, right? Not necessarily. Japan tried this. They pumped the equivalent of hundreds of billions of dollars into their economy in the '90s and lowered interest rates to nearly 0 percent. Do you think it worked? You're right, it did not. Many of their consumers had entered the saving phase of their lives, and nothing the government did could jolt them into spending more.

A major difference between Japan and the US is their population growth. Japan had discouraged family growth and did not have a new generation coming along behind their baby boomers that was large enough to grow their economy. Unfortunately, at this writing, the Japanese have not yet fully recovered from this economic cycle.

Demographers have called the baby boom generation "the pig in the python" because when viewed statistically, it represents a bulge in an otherwise skinny age distribution that gradually moves down the distribution as the boomers grow older. At this writing, it is reasonable to assume that we are in for a few years of slow, declining economic conditions.

Does this mean that you should not invest for growth? Not exactly. It means you need to have a plan that takes the overall situation into account. From 1985 to 2007, the buy-and-hold mantra was a chant that was growing in resonance among financial advisors (see chapter 1). However, most of them came to realize after the major stock market declines of 2001, 2002, 2008, and the beginning of 2009 that buy and hold wasn't working. Anyone who might have hung on to that antiquated notion is probably regretting it now as we endure another market recession. In the current investing environment, flexibility is crucial. If you have created an income plan and are considering how to invest your funds, you may want to look at it differently than you have in the past. So what is the right way to invest? In today's economic climate, there is no one-and-only "right" way.

As you talk to financial advisors, ask them what their opinions are about the economy and the stock market. If they do not have an opinion or if they seem to be giving you broad, sweeping statements, I would encourage you to look for another advisor.

It is typical for some financial professionals to absolve themselves of accountability and rely on a formulaic approach like 60 percent stocks/40 percent bonds. These are the same advisors who tell you to "just hang in there" when the account starts to lose money because of a severe market downturn. You need to have a proactive advisor who studies the conditions of the market on a daily basis and has a flexible investing philosophy that allows you to adjust to changing market conditions.

Knowledge and Wisdom

The more educated we are about the economy and how it is likely to move, the better we can plan financially. While some investors lost as much as half their fortunes in the market tailspin of 2008, there were some who lost very little. The reason? They were able to see things that others could not see.

Once, a teacher asked a high school class to write a term paper on the difference between knowledge, understanding, and wisdom.

"Knowledge," one student wrote, "is a collection of data and an accumulation of facts that you learn about something. Knowledge is information obtained through experience, observation, study, and research."

"Understanding," she continued, "is insight. It is fully grasping what we know and seeing what the facts really mean and how they relate to each other."

"Wisdom," she concluded, "is the ability to discern and judge which aspects of our collection of knowledge are applicable to our lives and apply that knowledge in a way that is beneficial to our well-being."

That student got an A.

But the only A+ in the class went to a young man who came up with the following succinct illustration:

"Knowledge is being aware that you are standing on a railroad track and a train is coming," he wrote.

"Understanding," he continued, "is grasping the relationship of those facts to each other. The train is hard steel. Your body is soft tissue. An impact would be fatal."

"Wisdom is getting off the tracks."

Whoever came up with the aphorism "Knowledge Is Power" was right, of course. But our knowledge is only power to the extent that we understand the facts and possess the wisdom to take the appropriate action.

CHAPTER 7

The Simple Truth about Annuities

Why is it when some people hear the word *annu-ity*, they clutch their chests and utter an audible gasp as if they just heard a bad word? I have seen some pretty intelligent people who usually have open minds, great cognitive skills, and the capacity to arrive at logical conclusions by examining the facts lose all of those attributes the instant the word *annuity* is brought up. As kids these days like to say, "What's up with that?"

I think it's due to what I call the *bad experience syndrome*. I know folks who have had a bad experience flying and they have vowed to never again board an airplane. No matter what you tell them or show them, either from a statistical viewpoint or an engineering viewpoint, they are convinced that strapping themselves into the seat of an airplane would be suicidal.

One person I know has to have his doctor give him a prescription for a powerful sedative before he flies. Personally, I don't get that. To convince yourself that flying is as safe as any other mode of travel, all you have to do is hang out at a busy airport for a day and watch the planes come and go, one after another, without incident. But you know what they say: "Feelings are facts." That fear of flying is very real to the person feeling it, no matter how irrational it may be.

Some have had bad experiences with annuities, particularly if they were talked into one by an aggressive salesperson who didn't explain exactly how an annuity works. Perhaps they had a bad experience with an insurance company, or maybe they saw one of those hidden-camera news specials that villainized annuities as all bad, all the time. Whatever the reason, it's easy to see why some draw back and cover their eyes when annuities are mentioned. Annuities have gotten some horrible press. But most people have a blank slate when it comes to annuities; they don't know much about them. So let's fix that, shall we? And not to persuade, but to educate.

In my experience, most of the negativity surrounding annuities tends to be about salespeople. Some unscrupulous insurance agents who obviously had dollar signs in their eyes instead of the best interests of their clients at heart have been caught on camera glossing over important details, telling direct lies, or stretching the truth just to make a sale. In one case

I know of, the salesperson didn't exactly lie; they just failed to inform the client that the product was completely unsuitable for them. Do you find that sort of thing distasteful? Who wouldn't? It's like selling auto insurance to someone who has no car. Please!

But that doesn't mean that car insurance is a bad thing. In fact, most Americans own car insurance and view it as a necessity. Similarly, there are lots of folks who are completely satisfied with their annuities. They love getting an income they can't outlive while they earn an attractive interest rate on their assets. When a market crash occurs, annuity owners are often the happiest of campers because their fixed annuities don't lose a dime. They may even have to resist a smug smile when they hear friends bemoan how much their portfolios lost when a market correction comes along and sweeps Wall Street clean like a stiff broom.

The popularity of annuities is indisputable. Billions of dollars are invested in them each year. *Somebody* has to be buying them. According to the Secure Retirement Institute (SRI), total sales of annuity products reached $242 billion in 2019. Variable annuity sales hit $102 billion, and fixed annuity sales came in at $140 billion. That marks an incredible shift in annuity understanding—one that I am very pleased with. Not long ago in a previous edition of this book, the numbers were essentially reversed. But people are realizing the value of fixed annuities (FIAs), especially fixed index annuities, which we will explore in greater detail later in this chapter. FIA sales have soared in recent years, reaching just shy of $74 billion in 2019. None of this could happen if all annuities are all bad, all the time; people vote with their dollars. Unscrupulous salespeople, however, are like rats, roaches, and ants—hard to exterminate completely without throwing the baby out with the bathwater. What follows are, as Joe Friday used to say on *Dragnet*, "just the facts, ma'am."

First of All, What Is an Annuity?

The word *annuity* derives from the Latin root *annu* or *annus*, which means "yearly." We get our English words *annual* and *anniversary* from the same root. Nothing too scary about that.

An annuity is a contract purchased by an individual from an insurance company. An annuity is an investment vehicle usually used to secure retirement income that pays a fixed number of payments over a set time period. As with any contract, the specific details are—you guessed it—in the wording of the contract. While the basic concept is the same, not all annuities are created equal—not by a long shot! To think that all annuities are the same would be like assuming that all automobile insurance policies are the same.

Three ways annuities can vary

1. Is it fixed rate or variable? This determines how money is invested in the annuity.

2. Do you want income now or later? This establishes whether the income is deferred or immediate.

3. Is the annuity single premium or flexible? This determines whether additional funds can be added to the investment.

Four parties to an annuity

The insurer. An annuity is always an agreement between you and an insurance company. This applies whether you buy the annuity from an independent agent or a bank or directly from the insurance company. Your money is invested according to your instructions and the type of annuity (fixed rate or variable, immediate or deferred). The insurer is governed by the details of the contract, which outlines what can and cannot be done with the investment. The contract spells out guarantees and cancellation penalties, as well as rules governing deposits and withdrawals.

The contract owner. The contract owner is the person who has invested in the annuity. The annuity owner:

- Provides the money for the investment.
- Chooses who the other parties of the contract will be.
- Signs the application and agrees to abide by the terms of the contract.

- Can withdraw money from the contract (according to the terms).
- Is responsible for any taxes that are due when such withdrawals are made.
- May add funds to the investment (if a flexible premium annuity).
- May terminate the agreement.
- May change beneficiaries.
- Is responsible for selecting from the contract options available.

In addition to those things, the owner of the annuity may change beneficiaries as well as the ownership named in the contract. Individuals, couples, partnerships, corporations, and trusts may legally be contract owners. The original owner can gift or will all or part of the contract to any individual or entity they choose.

The annuitant. This is where it can be a little confusing because the annuitant can be the contract owner, but does not have to be. The annuitant can be anyone—you, a spouse, a parent, a child, or another relative. The annuitant must be an individual, so it cannot be a trust, corporation, or partnership. The annuitant is like the insured in a life insurance policy. With life insurance, if the person who is insured dies, then the contract terminates. With an annuity, the annuitant is the *measuring life* of the contract— the person during whose life an annuity is payable.

So until the contract owner makes a change, or until the person named as annuitant dies, the terms of the annuity remain in force.

The beneficiary. The beneficiary of an annuity is similar to beneficiaries of other investments. Upon the annuitant's death, the beneficiary receives the inheritance. The beneficiary cannot change or control the contract. He or she has no say in how funds are invested. The beneficiary only benefits from an annuity upon the annuitant's death. A beneficiary can be a child, spouse, friend, relative, trust, corporation, or partnership. An annuity can have multiple beneficiaries with varying percentages payable to each that total 100 percent. The contract owner can change beneficiaries at any time; the consent of a beneficiary is not necessary.

Types of Annuities

There are two main types of annuities: *immediate* and *deferred*. Your income needs and desired flexibility will help determine which annuity type you choose. Do you want income now or in a few years? Do you want access to a lump sum of money? Would you like the largest possible income? These are just a few of the questions you would need to think through before purchasing an annuity.

Immediate annuity

If you purchase an immediate annuity, you are essentially trading a lump sum of money for an income stream. For example, you may give an insurance company $100,000 in return for $500 per month for the rest of your life—regardless of how long you live. The amount of income would be based on your current age and possibly your health.

You also could have payments sent to you for a specified number of years. The amount of income would be based on interest rates and the number of years you want income. In any case, you can have the checks sent to you monthly, quarterly, semi-annually, or annually.

Many of my clients and potential clients do not like this type of annuity because they feel they lose too much control. Once you have traded your lump sum of money for an income stream, the insurance company does not allow access to the remaining funds.

Deferred annuity

Most people purchase an annuity to grow their money rather than turn current funds into a lifetime income stream. The flexibility of deferred annuities, whether fixed or variable, is their main attraction. Deferred annuities offer guarantees for income planning, but the contract owner can decide to start or stop the income stream at any time. The contract could allow the money to simply grow (without withdrawals), or it could allow the owner to withdraw interest earned or principal.

With deferred annuities, there are three ways to grow the money. You can purchase a fixed rate, variable, or fixed index annuity. These types of annuities can be set up for a short or long period of time. The earnings in the account can be taken out or automatically reinvested for future growth.

With most deferred annuities, there is a period of time during which the funds can be subject to "surrender charges." These charges are incurred only if funds are withdrawn in excess of the free withdrawal percentage. Most annuities allow the owner to withdraw up to 10 percent each year without incurring a surrender charge. The surrender charge period is stated in the contract and is typically five to ten years. The surrender charge gradually decreases to zero over the specified period. There are some annuities available that have no surrender charges.

Deferred Annuity Investment Types

As I mentioned earlier, there are three ways for money to be invested in a deferred annuity: *fixed rate*, *variable*, and *fixed index*. Let's look at the basics of each.

Fixed rate annuities

Like other fixed rate products, a fixed rate annuity provides the contract owner with a guaranteed rate of return. These are similar to bank CDs (although CDs are FDIC insured and annuities are not). When you purchase a CD from a bank, the interest you receive usually depends on the time commitment; the longer the commitment, the higher the interest rate. A fixed rate annuity operates in a similar way. And, just like banks, some insurance companies offer higher rates than others.

The most common time horizons for fixed rate annuities are one, three, and five years. When you invest in a CD, the interest rate is locked in for a specified time. The same is true with a fixed rate annuity. The interest the annuity earns can be sent to the contract owner or reinvested to take advantage of compound interest.

Fixed rate annuities are popular with individuals who want to keep their principal safe. With this type of annuity, you will know exactly what to expect each year in interest. Fixed rate annuities work well for conservative investors or those who want to know exactly what they will have earned at the end of a specific time frame.

Variable annuities

For individuals who have a higher risk tolerance, variable annuities offer an alternative. With a variable annuity, you control how your funds are invested. Under the umbrella of tax-deferred annuities, investment options usually include many types of mutual funds. The contract owner can allocate and re-allocate his or her money from mutual fund to mutual fund. (However, some annuity contracts limit the frequency of movements.)

With a variable annuity, you typically are investing in the stock market or in bonds; therefore, there is a risk of loss. If the investment does well, you receive all the benefit, minus any fees. If the investment performs poorly, you can lose gains and even principal. There are several fees associated with a variable annuity. Most have mortality expenses, mutual fund fees, and surrender fees. These fees can vary from one annuity to another and can be very costly. They can also come as a big surprise if you are unaware of how they are charged.

Fixed index annuities

Fixed index annuities are a hybrid product. They combine the safety of principal offered by a fixed rate annuity with the market earnings potential of a variable annuity. Interest earnings are linked to a market index (such as the S&P 500, Dow, NASDAQ, Russell 2000, EURO STOXX 50, etc.). Fixed index annuities have been offered in the US since the mid-1990s. They have all the features of most fixed rate annuity contracts except that the interest earned is determined by the performance of the index to which the annuity is linked.

Most fixed index annuities use multiple formulas to calculate the interest to be credited. A popular crediting method is the "annual point-to-point with an interest cap." As the name implies, the annual point-to-point method calculates interest between two points each year—one at the beginning of the contract year and another at the end. The interest cap is the maximum you can earn in a given year.

For example, suppose you invested $100,000, and the interest crediting was linked to the S&P 500. Suppose the S&P 500 on the date you purchased the annuity (the first point) was valued at 1,000. One year later on your contract anniversary (the second point), the S&P 500 is valued at 1,100. By doing some simple math, you will find that the index has gained 10 percent. Let's assume the interest cap is 6 percent. The interest credited to your account will be 6 percent of $100,000, or $6,000, making your account balance $106,000. This amount becomes your base, and your account can never go below $106,000 unless you withdraw funds.

But wait a minute! The market rose 10 percent, and I only got 6 percent!

Yes, that is the trade-off. What could happen the following year? There is nothing to prevent the market from losing 30 percent, is there? Even if the index declines the following year, your base is protected. The worst you can do in a year is make 0 percent. This protection is why fixed index annuities have been popular with investors as of late.

One main detraction of fixed index annuities is their complication. There are some moving parts in this financial instrument. There are several methods for calculating interest, for example. The fine print is not necessarily damning, there is just a lot of it. Complexity has steered many investors away from these annuities. If you decide to use a fixed index annuity, I recommend choosing one that is easy for you to understand and making sure your advisor explains it thoroughly. If you are moving a large amount of money—and if that money represents years of your hard work, blood, sweat, toil, and tears—then make sure you understand where you are putting it and why you are putting it there. You should be as comfortable with that decision as you are that your left foot is in your left shoe. Make sure your advisor explains all the details and is able to support—in writing—the answers to all of your questions.

Income and Death Benefit Riders

Some insurance companies allow a contract owner to attach different *riders* to an annuity at the time of purchase. Riders add additional terms or provisions to the annuity contract. Most come with an annual fee.

One popular rider is a death benefit rider. These come in different forms based on the contract. Some insure the principal at the death of the annuitant regardless of market declines. For example, suppose you invested $100,000. Due to market declines, the value had dropped to $75,000 at your, the annuitant's, time of death. This version of the death benefit rider would pay the beneficiary the amount invested ($100,000) minus any prior withdrawals. There are also versions of the death benefit rider that guarantee an actual growth rate on the initial investment.

Another popular rider protects the contract owner's income. It provides peace of mind because in the event that the market declines, their income base will not. This type of rider is a good option to consider if you are planning for retirement and trying to ensure income for your basic needs.

Both riders and variable annuities have many different options and fees associated. It is important that you understand exactly how they work. Ask specific questions and get specific answers. Ask to see the explanation in writing. Your agent should be able to point out most of the answers in the annuity prospectus or contract paperwork.

Which Annuity Is Right for You?

The majority of your decisions regarding annuities will be based on your specific income needs and how you want your money invested. If you need the largest possible income immediately, then you likely will want to consider an immediate annuity. As for deferred annuities, there are many options. Don't let that overwhelm you. Work with an advisor you trust—one who will be patient and answer all of your questions.

The fact is that fixed rate, variable, and fixed index annuities are all very popular. The type that is best for you will depend on your time horizon, your other current investments, your goals and objectives, and your personal risk tolerance level.

As all investments do, annuities have pros and cons. One of the big complaints about annuities is that some have high fees and pay large commissions. This is true in some cases, but there are annuities that have extremely low costs, pay no commissions, and have no surrender charges. Take your time and clearly know why you are choosing a particular investment vehicle. I believe annuities can be very useful if they are used correctly and in the right circumstances.

CHAPTER 8

How to Determine Your Tolerance for Risk

Imagine for a moment that you are on a road trip. Someone else is driving. You are in the passenger seat. You learn very quickly that your life is in danger. The driver is paying no attention to the speed limit signs that whiz by as you fly down the road. This insane speed demon has the pedal to the metal and keeps it there, changing lanes erratically, blowing by other cars on the highway as if they are standing still. Despite your loud protests, the speedometer is still pegging 100 and more. You are trapped. This could last for hours if Speed Racer here doesn't kill you both. How do you feel? Scared? Out of control?

Now reverse the mental picture. You are in the passenger seat again, but this time the driver is moving very slowly along a busy interstate highway. Cars are zipping past, honking their horns, and it feels like you are sitting still. Now you are in a different kind of danger. Any minute now you just know someone is going to ram your car from behind and cause a chain reaction pileup. How would you like to be trapped for hours with Mr. Turtle behind the wheel? Pretty miserable, eh?

I think you know what I'm getting at. When we talk about risk tolerance, we're dealing with an individual comfort level. Can you be so aggressive with your investments that you endanger your livelihood? Of course, you can. Just ask investors who had all their assets riding the technology wave back in the late '90s, only to see the dot-com bubble burst and leave them broke. I know some daredevils back in that era who were trading with borrowed money and scooping up any stock that ended in .com. Then when the bubble burst, they were left deeply in debt.

I also know a few who don't trust banks, the stock market, insurance companies, or even Grandmother when it comes to their money. I will never forget a conversation I had with one gentleman who exhibited this kind of thinking. In the course of our interview, he told me that he kept his money buried in his backyard. He was smiling when he said it, so I took it as a joke. But as it turns out, the man wasn't joking. He had large sums of cash in glass jars, buried three feet deep at an undisclosed (at least to me) location on his farm.

I have also read about people who bought houses and found hundreds of thousands of dollars stashed in the walls. The *Cleveland Plain Dealer* once reported a case where an Ohio contractor named Bob Kitts was renovating an old house when he found $182,000 of Depression-era cash inside the walls of a bathroom. It turned out that the home's original owner was a wealthy businessman who hid money in the walls of his home rather than putting it in the banks, which he did not consider safe (and probably with good reason) at the time. That's what I call being ultraconservative with your investments.

How do you view investment risk? Investing in the stock market nearly always includes the *possibility* of losing some or all of the original investment. Think about that. It is true that professional money managers are able to calculate such things as the standard deviation of historical market returns in a specific area of investment and then tell you whether an investment is *comparatively* and *relatively* safe. A high standard deviation indicates a high degree of risk and vice versa. But in the end, there is always the possibility that you could lose the entire amount you invested.

Many companies these days pump large amounts of money, effort, and time into producing "risk management strategies" to help them manage the risk associated with their businesses and investments. If you are an investor who is in or approaching retirement, you should also assess your risk exposure. Some cavalierly pass this responsibility off to someone else. The events of 2008 should tell us, however, that just because someone has your portfolio doesn't mean they have your back. It is ultimately your responsibility to know where your assets are positioned. It is up to you to determine whether you are comfortable with the contingencies that could possibly arise from where your assets are placed.

So again, how do you personally feel about risk? That is your risk tolerance, and no one but you can measure it. I know some individuals who use the "sleep test." They feel that if they can go to bed and get a good night's rest, they are content with where their money is parked and how they have their resources situated. If they pace the floors at night nervously about a decision they made the previous day, then obviously the needle on their risk meter is over in the red zone and they need to retreat to a safer position.

Risk Perception Influenced by Experience

How you view risk will likely be influenced by your experiences in life. One thing my wife, Lauren, and I love to do is have good friends over for dinner. We are all busy people around our house, and most of our friends are busy, too, so we don't get the opportunity to host dinners as often as we would like. But when we do, we find stimulating conversation around the table, or in what Lauren calls the "conversation pit" of our living room. Through this quite enjoyable pastime, I have noticed something about conversations. If they ever lag, all it takes to re-ignite the spark is a good question posed to the group. I have some stock questions to toss out if the conversation seems to tire. They include:

"Who's the most famous person you ever personally met?"

"What's the most money you have ever found?" You get some interesting stories out of that one. I'm always envious because the most I have ever found was a five-dollar bill in an old coat I was getting ready to throw away.

But the one I like to ask that gets the most interesting responses is "What is the riskiest, or most dangerous, situation in which you have ever found yourself?"

Some of my friends, come to find out, have been lost in caves, chased by bears, almost drowned, and had all sorts of other close calls.

"It's a wonder I'm still here," someone will always say.

One common thread I have discovered in all their stories is that most of them happened when they were young. Isn't it true that when we are young, we feel as if we are bulletproof and can leap tall buildings with a single bound? It's no wonder, then, that we take greater chances with life and limb. But once we have a little more mileage on us, we are less apt to so casually place ourselves in harm's way. It's not so much that we are wiser, although that's certainly part of it. Experience has taught us our limitations.

What about those people who got burned by Bernie Madoff's multi-billion-dollar Ponzi scheme a few years back? Do you think they will ever again be so gullible? Will they ever be pulled in by the lure of high returns with little risk? I doubt it.

Have you ever lost money or been taken advantage of by someone who used tricks, lies, or misleading information? Then you were no doubt schooled by the situation and will never again be so unsuspecting. As my mother always says, "Once burned, twice shy," only "burned" comes out "burnt."

Bottom line: Risk tolerance is an individual thing. Some love the way the stock market works, while others may get physically sick at the thought of its volatility. Some may have a great pension that provides secured income regardless of how long they live, while others may not have any secured income and will not likely relish the idea of placing what they do have in the way of any risk, regardless of the potential rewards. How likely are you to want to place a non-renewable, irreplaceable resource at risk? I'm going to go out on a limb and say not likely. Think water in the desert.

There are individuals who, throughout their lives, have never experienced any great financial losses.

They may feel very comfortable with risk. I call it the *Midas touch syndrome.* You remember King Midas from your studies of Greek mythology in high school, don't you? Everything he touched turned to gold. Some people seem to lead charmed lives when it comes to their investments. They get in at the right time and get out at the right time. They avoid the downturns and ride the upturns. It's not that they are all that brilliant. They seem to exemplify that old adage: "I would rather be lucky than smart any day of the week." But like most Las Vegas lucky streaks, such good fortune doesn't usually continue if you stay too long at the table. That's one reason why, as a financial advisor, I prefer the more measured, logical approach of statistical analysis coupled with a sell-side discipline. I like to think of the stock market as neither a friend nor a foe but a territory to be explored carefully with plenty of safeguards built in so that you are never in danger and you never get lost.

This "road trip" called retirement will have a few main intersections where your risk tolerance meter will have to be involved. The way you view risk will determine how you make decisions and which course you take. In its most general terms, risk tolerance represents a trade-off between fear and greed. As you make investment decisions and choices, you will find yourself doing a balancing act with regret—regretting the losses incurred by taking too much risk and regretting the gains lost by taking too little.

Psychometric Testing

As I've said before, feelings are facts. That is certainly true when it comes to risk tolerance, which is essentially how you feel about risk. But how can risk tolerance be measured? How do you gauge your own personal risk comfort zone? It is not an easy task because it may be like trying to hit a moving target.

Here's what I mean: Suppose you were in a bad car wreck last week. Because of that, your level of caution today likely is much higher than usual. You may not even be able to drive or ride in a car yet. But as the trauma of the accident fades with time, you likely will return to normal and begin driving again, albeit gradually and with a good deal more caution than before—especially at first. Asked to describe your driving during that initial return to the wheel, an observer would no doubt label it "very cautious." But that assessment would be skewed—affected by the aftermath of the trauma of a serious accident. The same is true in other areas of your life. More details and background information are needed in order to form a complete picture of one's risk tolerance.

This leads us to an area of psychological testing known as *psychometrics*. Breaking down that word to its most basic parts, we get *psycho* meaning "of the mind" and *metric* meaning "to measure." From that, we can infer that this branch of psychology helps us measure the mind. Psychometric testing can be used to measure attitudes, personality traits, abilities, and knowledge. These measures are typically taken by means of analyzing answers to questions on questionnaires or other tests designed to assess attitudes and responses.

Some financial analysts use a psychometric test in an effort to acquire a more accurate reading of a client's risk tolerance. You won't see these psychometric tests come right out and ask, "How do you view risk?" That would be too obvious. The questions take a subtler approach, asking about your preferences, values, and attitudes in general. These tests approach the question of risk tolerance sideways, true, but they are surprisingly accurate. The reason why psychometric tests approach risk in general terms is to avoid skewed answers.

A good test must be both valid (i.e., it measures what it is supposed to measure) and reliable (i.e., it measures risk tolerance not only accurately, but also consistently). For example, a test to determine temperature would involve a thermometer. To check the accuracy of the reading, another thermometer of the same calibration could be used, and the reading should be exactly the same if used under the same conditions. A psychometric test will be designed to achieve the same results regardless of what order the questions are asked in or how they are phrased.

A good test will also have questions written in plain English and will avoid the use of financial terms that may be confusing. There should be a minimum of

20 questions so that results will be statistically relevant. The firms that develop these tests should be able to provide ample evidence that the test meets all professional psychometric testing standards.

What Can a Risk Tolerance Test Reveal?

I believe the answers you give to a risk tolerance test will help you understand your financial self better. If you are part of a couple investing together, both you and your partner should take the test. Doing so will provide a clearer picture of your attitudes about financial risk and your partner's as well. Married individuals often have different levels of risk tolerance.

One of the things I like to do when I first begin working with clients is get to know them from a risk tolerance perspective. The comments of one memorable couple were quite revealing on the matter when I asked how they would rate their own tolerance for risk on a scale of 1 to 10, with 1 being ultraconservative and 10 being very inclined to take risks.

"Ten," blurted the husband, adding "You know what they say: NO PAIN, NO GAIN."

His wife, sitting next to him, gave him a wicked look and kicked his shin. "Three," she said. "No, make that two."

For some reason, the title of John Gray's book about male/female disparity, *Men Are from Mars, Women Are from Venus*, came to mind.

When it comes to money and risk, that couple's opposing responses are more typical than you may know. Each partner in a relationship may be able to say who is more risk averse or risk tolerant, but they often aren't aware of how wide the disparity is—or why the disparity exists—without getting a professional assessment. Reviewing a detailed risk profile report can offer that big-picture view of your differences.

Knowing how and why you and your partner differ financially will help you understand each other better. It will also help you make better joint financial decisions—decisions with which you both will be more comfortable. Add to the mix a competent financial planner who can offer several alternative strategies, and you will be able to negotiate your way to a peaceful and amicable settlement even on the stickiest of issues.

No, a financial advisor cannot make decisions for you on matters of risk tolerance. But what a good financial advisor can do is help you make decisions that enable each of you to stay within your comfort zones.

How Your Financial Advisor Assesses Risk Tolerance

To what extent are you prepared to risk a less favorable outcome by pursuing a more favorable outcome? What is it they say? "Nothing ventured, nothing gained"? Well, that may be a cliché, but most of us recognize the universal truth in its meaning. How much will you risk in order to gain? Good question.

But you have to determine where on the spectrum you are psychologically comfortable in order to set the balance between fear and greed. You might call this balance point your "financial comfort zone." Below it, you're taking too few risks and may feel you are missing out on opportunities. Go above it, and you're taking on too much risk; you may be plagued with anxiety and worry. You want to avoid both of these extremes.

That's why it is essential that your financial advisor gets as good an understanding as possible of your risk tolerance. While some advisors are good at this, it is an unfortunate truth that others are not. From where I observe the financial advisory profession, the average advisor is significantly more risk tolerant than the average client. That shouldn't be a problem if advisors refuse to allow their personal opinions to influence the advice they provide to clients. Let me put it this way: it is unprofessional for your advisor to suggest investments to you based on *his or her* personal risk tolerance.

Whether you are seeking a new advisor or talking with your current advisor, to see where you stand on this issue, try this: Ask them to explain to you how they view your risk tolerance. Ask them how they came to their conclusions about it. Did they use any type of psychometric testing to help define your risk aversion? If so, did they use standardized tests, and can the publisher of the test prove its scientific validity?

When your financial advisor suggests strategies and solutions, make sure they fall within your financial comfort zone. Your advisor should be able to provide alternatives that meet your personal level of risk tolerance, no matter what it is.

Risk Tolerances Change over Time

Because your tolerance for risk will change over time, your financial plan cannot be a set-it-and-forget-it plan. You must review your plan on a regular basis because time changes everything. Even if you are healthy, you will see a doctor on an annual basis for a checkup. Why? To see if everything is still all right. As you get older, this becomes more important than ever. There may come a point in time when in order to keep that good health, you may have to begin watching your weight more carefully. Your cholesterol or your blood pressure may tick up, requiring changes in your overall physical routine. In the same way, your risk tolerance should be reviewed regularly. Life events can influence it. Any major life event—good or bad, happy or sad—should trigger a risk tolerance review. Otherwise, a review at least every two or three years is appropriate.

Learn how you and your spouse view risk. Ask your advisor how he or she assesses clients' risk aversion. Have a thorough understanding of your risk tolerance before and throughout your retirement.

This knowledge will aid you tremendously in having peace of mind about your retirement plan and your investments.

CHAPTER 9

How to Find a Financial Professional You Can Trust

Do you know your advisor?

"Know my advisor? What does that mean? Of course, I know my advisor. I even know his golf handicap!" That's not what I mean. Of course, you know your advisor's name, where his or her office is located. You may know your advisor's family. Heck, you may even be related to your advisor's family. I just think you should know more—like exactly how your advisor gets paid and what your advisor's responsibility is to you. Do you know those things?

Is your advisor held to a fiduciary standard? Is there a system in place to communicate with you regularly? Do you have a written document called an Investment Policy Statement? Let's tackle these things one at a time.

Commissions and Fees

It's a funny thing about professional people and the air they sometimes project. When you go to the doctor's office, does the person behind the glass enclosure ever look up, smile, wave at you, get up and come around the counter to shake your hand, congratulate you for being on time, and tell you that the doctor will see you right away? Didn't think so.

More often than not, you are greeted nonchalantly, if at all. You must tell them who you are and why you are there. The front desk attendant checks to make sure you have a right to be there and then tells you to have a seat. This really should not surprise us. It is, after all, called a "waiting room." Even though you were prompt, you are asked to wait and read a magazine or fiddle with your phone.

Ready for a paradigm shift? The doctor *works for you*. Yes, as skilled as he or she may be, as nice a bedside manner as he or she may have, and as protected as he or she may be by the cadre of white-coated guards out front, the truth is the doctor works for you. You pay the bill. Whether through your insurance premiums or directly from your pocket, you are the one who picks up the tab for the doctor's services. But we do have respect for the doc's education and status as an expert. And so out of deference for that, and since we are completely intimidated by the time-honored ritual to the point of lamb-like submission, we do not dare act as if we are in charge of this little exercise. Which is why we would never, never question how much the good doctor charges for his or her services. We meekly pay the charges and defer to what I call the "air of professionalism" that is cast like an ethereal vapor by the visage of a white coat and a stethoscope.

Do you think this is also why we don't dare ask how our financial advisor gets paid? Is that question just considered too inappropriate and impertinent to ask of a professional? It shouldn't be. I have people come into my office all the time and tell me they have been with a certain advisor for a few years. They say they like and trust them. Then I ask them how their advisor gets paid. Most do not know. They assume their advisor gets paid by the mutual fund or the annuity company. Some say they pay their advisor a fee, and others say their advisor receives some combination of commission and fees. When I ask what the fee is, most do not know! You should ask. You should know.

Why is it important that you know how your advisor is compensated? Consider this: If your advisor only receives a commission when he or she sells you something or makes changes to your mutual funds, how might that influence his or her recommendations? Is it possible that a profit motive could enter into the decision? If your advisor is paid by fee only, how much is the fee? Who pays it, and what comprises the fee?

How and how often is it charged? Would knowing the answer to those questions affect the level of confidence you have in your advisor's recommendations?

If you are interviewing a new advisor, make sure you ask about compensation right up front. If the advisor is trying to sell you a product that earns him or her a commission, you should know that. Don't misunderstand me. I am by no means saying that commissions are wrong. I am sure the travel agency I occasionally deal with makes a commission from the airlines when they book flights for me. Under no circumstances do I think they are playing favorites with one particular airline over another because of that. I have seen them clicking away at their computer keyboards, trying to squeeze out the best fare for me and make sure that I am traveling at the most convenient time with the least possible hassle. I am confident that they do not give their commissions a thought. But that's how they get paid.

What I am saying is that if you understand how your advisor gets paid, then you can ask why he or she recommended a particular product, service, or strategy. It's okay to ask how much the commission was. To misquote a line from *The Godfather*, "It's business, not personal."

If your current advisor, or the candidate you are interviewing for the job, does not seem willing to answer the question about compensation clearly and quickly, that could be an indication that you may want to look elsewhere.

Is Your Advisor Held to a Fiduciary Standard?

In the financial services industry, there are brokers and there are advisors. There are people who sell products and people who sell knowledge. There are people who look out for their commissions and people who look out for you. The difference is a **fiduciary standard**. *Merriam-Webster* defines fiduciary as "held or founded in trust or confidence." A fiduciary standard is about *your* interests, *your* goals, and *your* well-being. Do you know if your financial advisor is held to a fiduciary standard? If they are to protect you and your financial livelihood, they should be.

Do you expect your doctor or lawyer to put your interests first? Of course, you do; doctors and lawyers are held to a fiduciary standard. That almost goes without saying. As for financial advisors, the fact is that many are not held to this high standard. Do you want your advisor to be required to put your interests first? If you currently have an advisor, ask if he or she is required by law to put your interests first. If you are interviewing an advisor, make sure he or she is held to a fiduciary standard before you agree to do business.

A registered investment advisor (RIA) is a person or company that has registered with the US Securities and Exchange Commission (SEC) or with a State Securities Division. This registration does not mean the SEC approves, sanctions, or attests to the merits of the person or company. It simply indicates the person or entity is registered and has agreed to abide by certain fiduciary standards. An RIA may be registered with a State Securities Division as well as with the SEC.

The RIA and Investment Advisor (IA) designations came about from the Investment Advisors Act of 1940. The fiduciary standard is based on the laws this act put in place. The fiduciary standard means that an advisor is *required* to act only in the best interest of his or her client. This is true even if the interest of the client conflicts with the advisor's financial interests. An advisor held to this standard is required to report any existing or potential conflicts of interest before and during the time the advisor is engaged by the client. Additionally, RIAs and IAs must disclose how they are compensated and agree to abide by a code of ethics. Very few who claim to be financial advisors are actually federally registered or state registered. Most are considered to be broker-dealers, who are, by designation, held to lower and non-regulated standards.

Federal law requires broker-dealers to act in the best interest of their *employers*—not their clients. This does not mean they are unethical or plan to harm their clients. In fact, I feel confident that most broker-dealers are ethical and do not intend harm to their clients. The scary thing is that they are not required by law to act in their clients' best interests. If your advisor is not required to act in your best interest, this limits your recourse if you feel you have been taken advantage of.

To guard against unethical violations, the SEC requires broker-dealers to include the following disclosure in their client agreements. Read this disclosure:

Your account is a brokerage account and not an advisory account. Our interests may not always be the same as yours. Please ask us questions to make sure you understand your rights and our obligations to you, including the extent of our obligations to disclose conflicts of interest and to act in your best interest. We are paid both by you and, sometimes, by people who compensate us based on what you buy. Therefore, our profits, and our salespersons' compensation, may vary by product and over time.

Is this the type of relationship you want with your advisor? If you have signed an agreement with an advisor, go look at it. Is this disclaimer in there? If so, ask your advisor for more details. Decide if the relationship is in your best interest.

What Is an Investment Policy Statement?

Do you have an investment policy statement (IPS)? What is it? An IPS is a written statement that details the policies, procedures, and goals you and your advisor have agreed to uphold in regard to managing your investments. This type of document is required when a fiduciary relationship exists.

An IPS outlines a systematic approach for making decisions. It establishes a way to tackle difficult issues related to your investment choices. Having a plan provides clarity as you work with your advisor to meet certain expectations and goals. A well-thought-out statement helps your advisor understand what you expect. It also demonstrates your advisor's willingness to meet your investment needs and help you meet your goals.

What should an IPS include? It is advisable to include the following sections in the IPS:

- **Objectives.** In clearly defined language, the IPS should describe expectations, risk tolerance, return decisions, and guidelines for investments.

- **Asset allocation policy.** This section will categorize the asset classes you want in your portfolio and define how those assets are best allocated to meet your goals.

- **Management procedures.** This should outline how you want your investments monitored and evaluated. It should detail how and when changes should be managed.

- **Communication procedures.** Good communication is essential when it comes to your investments. This section should detail communication processes and objectives for both client and advisor. It should also assign responsibility for implementation.

Certain steps are required to establish an investment policy:

1. Identify what your financial goals and needs are so you can determine your financial situation.

2. Establish your risk tolerance and your investment time horizon.

3. Set long-term investment goals.

4. Decide what restrictions you have for your portfolio and assets.

5. Determine the asset classes and allocation that will maximize the likelihood of achieving your investment objectives at the lowest level of risk.

6. Decide how you want to handle investment selection, rebalancing, buy-sell principles, portfolio reviews, reporting, and so on.

7. Implement the decisions and review as necessary.

Do you know what causes investors to make poor decisions most of the time? Two things: Lack of information and too little forethought. Emotions also play a part in poor decision-making. An IPS will provide investors with a written statement that can guide them in this regard. It is my belief that good investment decisions are the result of obtaining good, solid information through diligent research and applying logic supported by the numbers. An IPS is crucial in making prudent and rational investment decisions.

CERTIFIED FINANCIAL PLANNER™ Practitioner

Should your advisor be a CERTIFIED FINANCIAL PLANNER™ practitioner? Most likely the only one who would say no to this is an advisor who has not achieved the designation. Why should your advisor be one?

When people hear the term "financial planner," they believe that person surely must have some sort of certification or have undergone some level of training. In fact, that is not the case. Nearly anyone can get away with calling themselves a financial planner. However, it is only those who have fulfilled the requirements of the Certified Financial Planner Board of Standards who may use the CFP® certification mark. This mark can provide you with a sense of security in knowing that the person has met a baseline of training and preparation. The requirements, outlined in detail below, are a combination of education, exams, years of experience, and adherence to an ethical code.

Education. A CFP® practitioner must have a bachelor's degree from an accredited US college or university, or an equivalent foreign university. His or her studies must have included financial planning subject areas outlined by the CFP Board as necessary to become a competent financial planner. The subject areas encompass investment planning, income tax planning, insurance planning, employee benefits planning, risk management, and retirement and estate planning.

Examination. To earn the CFP® certification, the person must pass a comprehensive 10-hour exam (taken over two days). The exam includes scenarios and case studies that determine one's ability to diagnose financial planning issues and apply learned knowledge to real-world circumstances.

Experience. To become a CFP® practitioner, the person must have a minimum of three years of full-time financial planning experience. This must equate to 2,000 hours per year.

Ethics. The CFP Board has developed documents that detail the ethical and practice standards to be followed by CFP® professionals. Those with the CFP® certification agree to follow the Board's Standards of Professional Conduct.

After becoming certified, training is not over for a CFP®. To continue using the CFP® mark, these individuals must complete ongoing education and ethics training. This includes 30 hours of continuing education every two years. Two of those hours must be on the Code of Ethics and other parts of the Standards of Professional Conduct. This training is intended to ensure that CFP® professionals stay abreast of developments in the financial planning field.

Furthermore, CFP® professionals have to renew their agreement to abide by the Standards of Professional Conduct. A major aspect of this agreement requires that CFP® professionals provide financial planning services at a fiduciary standard of care. They must offer financial planning services that align with the best interests of their clients.

CFP® professionals who fail to meet these requirements can be suspended or have their certifications permanently revoked. For added confidence in the abilities of your financial advisor, I recommend that you consider working with a CFP® practitioner.

Act in Your Own Best Interest

There are other things to consider when choosing an advisor, but looking at the topics detailed in this chapter can be a great start. Choosing a competent financial advisor you trust may be one of the most important decisions you make. Not only can your choice impact your life, but it also can impact the lives of your loved ones.

Choose your advisor wisely. The right advisor can guide you and your family as you address specific financial concerns throughout your life. They can help you find financial peace of mind and assist you in achieving your lifelong goals. Never let an advisor scare you into becoming a client or make you feel guilty in order to keep you as a client. Take the time to get complete answers to all of your questions. Above all, act in your own best interest.

—